"Cory McCartney's *The Heisman Trophy* isn't a dry listing of facts but a living, breathing tribute to what makes the award so special. Well researched and flawlessly written. You will learn a lot. I know I did."
—Tony Barnhart, SEC Network, *Gridiron Now*

"Understanding the origins of our institutions, and the reluctant characters that comprise them, is central to our ability to be inspired and achieve more. It brings greatness within reach of all who seek it in our daily lives. Cory McCartney has done a masterful job of unpacking the history of the Heisman Trophy while leaving its patina which adds to the value of college football's currency: TRADITION!"
—Spencer Tillman, Sr. Analyst, FOX Sports 1; CEO, Axiom Sports Productions

"A must-read for college football nuts, *The Heisman Trophy: The Story of an American Icon and Its Winners* illustrates the rich tradition behind the most coveted award in sports. McCartney's storytelling sheds light on the trends and narratives that have shaped the Heisman's long history and offers a peek inside its exclusive fraternity of winners."
—Zac Ellis, Writer and Digital Media Editor at Vanderbilt Athletics

"*The Heisman Trophy: The Story of an American Icon and Its Winners* is a must-read for any college football fan. Cory's ability to go beyond the headlines and dive deep into the stories of some of the game's biggest stars is perfect for the casual fan and CFB buffs."
—Barrett Sallee, *Bleacher Report*

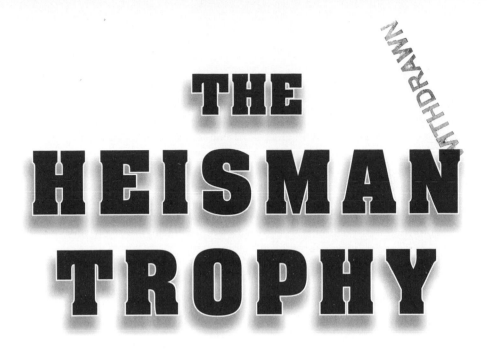

THE HEISMAN TROPHY

THE STORY OF AN AMERICAN ICON AND ITS WINNERS

CORY McCARTNEY

SPORTS
PUBLISHING

Sports Publishing books may be purchased in bulk at special discounts for sales promotion, corporate gifts, fund-raising, or educational purposes. Special editions can also be created to specifications. For details, contact the Special Sales Department, Sports Publishing, 307 West 36th Street, 11th Floor, New York, NY 10018 or sportspubbooks@skyhorsepublishing.com.

Sports Publishing® is a registered trademark of Skyhorse Publishing, Inc.®, a Delaware corporation.

Visit our website at www.sportspubbooks.com.

10 9 8 7 6 5 4 3 2 1

Library of Congress Cataloging-in-Publication Data

Names: McCartney, Cory, author.
Title: The Heisman Trophy : the story of an American icon and its winners / Cory McCartney.
Description: New York : Skyhorse Publishing, [2016]
Identifiers: LCCN 2016035167| ISBN 9781613219331 (Hardcover : alk. paper) | ISBN 9781613219348 (Ebook)
Subjects: LCSH: Football players--United States--Biography. | Heisman Trophy--History. | College sports--United States--History--20th century. | National Collegiate Athletic Association--History.
Classification: LCC GV939.A1 M43 2016 | DDC 796.332/63--dc23 LC record available at https://lccn.loc.gov/2016035167

Cover design by Tom Lau
Cover photo credit AP Images

Print ISBN: 978-1-61321-933-1
Ebook ISBN: 978-1-61321-934-8

Printed in the United States of America

TABLE OF CONTENTS

ACKNOWLEDGMENTS

IT STARTED WITH superheroes. As a kid, I was obsessed with these exaggerated ideals of human existence. A man could fly, run faster than a locomotive, and those buildings? He'd leap over them in a single bound.

But later Superman was replaced by Bo Jackson—who, ironically, had his own turn as a superhero alongside Wayne Gretzky and Michael Jordan in the Saturday morning cartoon *ProStars*. The exaggerated was no longer fictional, and Jackson ignited that flame, the ideal cast in bronze: a Heisman Trophy winner.

That torch was later carried by Barry Sanders and on and on, this stiff-armed statue becoming symbolic of that same infatuation with capes and tights. It was and is, as Heisman Trust president William J. Dockery would tell me, "an icon to the youth of America."

Its recipients' paths will always be dissected through a different lens than those of their contemporaries. Do they join the eight Heismen (Doak Walker, Paul Hornung, Roger Staubach, O. J. Simpson, Tony Dorsett, Earl Campbell, Marcus Allen, and Sanders) who would go on to Hall of Fame careers in the NFL? Are they considered part of an even longer lists of busts, a la Rashaan Salaam, Andre Ware, Gary Beban, and Gino Torretta? What makes the Heisman so powerful is that ultimately it doesn't matter. Whether they end up being considered as a legend or a flop, their receipt of the Heisman is likely to be the first line in any of their obituaries.

What follows in this book is the award in both brilliance and imperfection, as inspirational and divisive. In the annals of American sports, what other trophy can have that same impact?

None but the Heisman.

A special thank-you to my wife, Jama, and my sons, Jack and Cooper, for supporting me through a project I've longed to produce.

Thanks to Tim Henning with the Heisman Trust, the sports information directors who proved so helpful along the way—E. J. Borghetti (Pitt), Jerry Emig (Ohio State), Keith Mann (Nebraska), Heath Nielsen (Baylor), and Tim Tessalone (USC)—as well as Kent Stephens with the College Football Hall of Fame, Kelly Kline, Jay Berwanger biographer Brian Cooper, Gene Menez, who in our *Sports Illustrated* days opened the door for me to seize the reins of the Heisman coverage and to become a voter—and, of course, my editor, Julie Ganz, for helping to make this all possible.

INTRODUCTION

An Icon Is Born

"**I**'**VE ALWAYS BELIEVED** that the Heisman [Trophy] is a team award," said Archie Griffin, the only two-time winner.

"Because I don't care how great a player you are—on offense if you don't have that line clicking for you, making holes for you to run through, or as a quarterback if you don't have that offensive line protecting you to allow you to throw that ball the way you're capable of throwing it, it just doesn't happen."

The Heisman is a 25-pound icon-maker, going, as the plaque below the ballcarrier states, *TO THE OUTSTANDING COLLEGE FOOTBALL PLAYER IN THE UNITED STATES*. Every new winner becomes forever tied to the likes of Davey O'Brien, Roger Staubach, and Barry Sanders. By its very definition, the Heisman is the bronze embodiment of this country's golden boy spirit, not awarded to the team, but to a man.

Or, to modernize the connotation: *The Man.*

"Football is a team game, and I don't care how you slice it, you have to have a team really clicking to win the Heisman Trophy," Griffin said.

Funny thing about that stance, though: as the award's unmatched winner believes, so too did the Heisman's namesake, as well as the person who sculpted it. The concept of honoring the nation's best player was ultimately the brainchild of Willard B. Prince.

In 1935, John Heisman—the first athletic director of New York's Downtown Athletic Club, who had, in a famed coaching career, helped to bring the forward pass, handoff, and center snap to the game—was approached by Prince, the *D. A. C. Journal*'s first publisher and editor, about a trophy to recognize the game's best player.

"How about it, John?" Prince asked him. "We have this award and we name it after you?"

For Prince, the concept made sense. After an accomplished military career in which he was awarded the Silver Star and was the first American trained in aerial photography, he went into advertising. Prince saw the value not only in the debate that could come with such an award, but also what it could mean to the DAC, which was trying to separate itself from the city's other private clubs.

Heisman, though, was taken aback.

"No, no, no," he responded. "It's a team sport. You can't give it to an individual."

Heisman was, if anything, a stickler. The vagabond, who coached at eight schools—among them modern-day powers Auburn, Clemson, and Georgia Tech—wholly believed in fundamentals and discipline, saying upon his arrival at the University of Pennsylvania in 1920, "Eating a piece of pie may not be very detrimental to a man's physical condition, but irrevocably reduces the prestige of the team's morale. The captain of the team must be addressed by his title, and all the coaches must be called 'coach' while engaged in practice."

Breaking from those militaristic notions of a unit railed against everything Heisman preached as a coach, but Prince wouldn't let up.

In 1926, the lawyers and executives who created the DAC bought up land by the Hudson River (the site was the location of George Washington's farewell to the last meeting of Congress held in New York), dreaming of building an extravagant club. But the stock market crash stopped the group from buying any more land and they were forced to build a 45-story brick building on a plot of land so small that designers had to put the basketball court, tennis courts, pool, miniature golf course, driving range, and boxing ring on different floors.

The club was also burdened with debt and in need of members, so Heisman agreed to take Prince's idea to his monthly meeting with radio personalities and newspaper writers. They loved the idea of the award.

Heisman relented, though with one major caveat: his name would not in any way be attached to the trophy.

John Heisman relented to the Downtown Athletic Club singling out an individual player for its award, but didn't want his name attached to it.

Feeling that any traditional trophy wouldn't do to capture the kind of achievement it was attempting to embody, the DAC sought out a unique design and Willard Prince—whom club management put in charge of the trophy—brought in a number of the leading sculptors of the day. They all turned him down.

He instead found a twenty-three-year-old recent graduate of the Pratt Institute in Brooklyn, whose professional résumé included factory work making mannequins, dolls, and Easter bunnies.

"Whatever the job, it was always something where I could use some form of sculpting," Frank Eliscu told FineArt-e.com.

Eliscu's hands would create the likes of inaugural medals for President Gerald Ford and Vice President Nelson Rockefeller in 1974 and the "Cascade of Books" that sits atop the entrance to the James Madison Memorial Building of the Library of Congress.

The latter would be arguably his most celebrated work, a five-story-high bronze screen that consisted of ninety-eight open books. It weighs twenty-seven tons.

"All that is man, his hopes, his dreams, his aspirations, would never be known if not for the gift of books," Eliscu would say of his piece. "I wanted to create a work quietly evocative of the building's purpose, yet powerful enough so that it would not be just a decoration that the eye of the beholder would pass over without a second glance."

Yet, to the layman, Eliscu is best known not for that installation, his work on the statue of Thomas Jefferson for the Jefferson Memorial, or what he meant to the field of plastic surgery as an army sergeant, when he developed a technique of tattooing for removing birthmarks and aiding in lip reconstruction. His legacy revolves around something he did for his first commission, a sum of $200.

"He did much more significant things and that's what people remember," said Eliscu's daughter, Norma Eliscu Banas. "He was very young and it was not important to him at the time, and he was very pleased that he brought it recognition, but as an artist, he did much better pieces."

Long before he penned "Looks Like We Made It" or "Mandy," Barry Manilow wrote commercial jingles, including Band-Aid's "Stuck on Me." If Manilow's name conjured up that ad despite his string of number-one hits, that would be akin to what Eliscu experienced.

Or, as Eliscu himself explained in a 1982 interview, "It would be like trying to compare the golf game of Jack Nicklaus at age twelve to the golf game of Jack Nicklaus today."

The sculptor had been given just one piece of guidance from the DAC; they wanted a football player in action, and Eliscu created three four-inch wax mock-ups of different poses.

The DAC would send Heisman, Columbia's Lou Little, and Jim Crowley of Fordham—also a member of Notre Dame's fabled Four Horsemen backfield—as consultants to see what Eliscu had come up with, and all of them picked a straight-arm runner. But Eliscu's favorite was of a lineman tackling a ballcarrier, their bodies entangled into the shape of an S.

"He argued with them, and he did their pose," said Eliscu Banas.

But he did so with a twist. The three Hall of Famers felt the player's arm should be pointed to the side, a more natural position than the straight-back look that Eliscu had devised. He simply bent the pliable mold until the arm was in the requested spot. Heisman also insisted a smile Eliscu put on the sketch be replaced with a snarl and Crowley and Little pushed for fingers on the runner's extended hand be splayed out.

"If I had to do it a again, I'd make some changes," Eliscu told the *St. Petersburg Evening Independent*, forty-seven years after the fact. "I'd use different techniques and textures in the face and muscular structure."

He looked to a newspaper picture for some of the details—prophetically, it was of Jay Berwanger, who would become the trophy's first recipient—and more came from Eliscu's imagination as he formed clay around a wire frame. But when it came to the uniform, Eliscu wasn't willing to let artistic license lead him.

He called upon his friend Ed Smith—a running back at New York University who would later play for the NFL's Boston Redskins and Green Bay Packers—and asked him to bring his uniform to Eliscu's studio. Wearing his leather helmet, canvas pants, and high-top cleats, Smith posed for his high school friend, extending his right arm forward while cradling a ball with his left. It took nearly a month to complete the sculpture, with Smith posing multiple times.

"I really didn't know what it was for," Smith told the Associated Press in 1986. "He was looking for somebody who looked like a football player and he knew just what he wanted."

A month after those sessions, Eliscu had finished the sculptor in clay and took it to Crowley, who had one of his Fordham players, halfback Warren Mulrey, mimic the pose to ensure authenticity. The working model would go through its final inspection on November 16, 1935 at a dinner in the McAlpin Hotel with Notre Dame coach Elmer Layden and his entire team on hand.

The end result was fluid movement. A look of steely determination is across his face, while the left hand is gripped around the ball with the bicep curled; the right hand is readied to push away a would-be tackler. Legs muscles bulge as he strides ahead.

"That is good football," Eliscu said in 1977, "but it is not good sculpture because [the fingers] can be broken off too easily."

It was nearly fifty years later before Smith found out that the trophy carried his likeness, with Eliscu telling a documentary film crew in 1982. In the years following the discovery, the DAC invited Smith to the awards dinners and provided him with his own copy of the trophy.

As for Eliscu's original plaster cast, it sold in 2005—on the same day that Reggie Bush was awarded the seventy-first Heisman—fetching $271,360 in auction.

"This is the first time there will be two Heisman winners in one day," auction house Sotheby's director Lee Dunbar said at the time.

Days after the Fighting Irish had signed off on the pose, Prince sent ballots to writers east of the Mississippi River. His son John was seven at the time and recalls he, his sister (nine), and his brother (ten) helping to tally up the sixty-five votes.

"My dad put them in his briefcase, brought them home to Brooklyn, and set up a card table in the back parlor of this brownstone house and we counted ballots," said John Prince, now eighty-seven.

That was the only year that the Downtown Athletic Club didn't farm out the process to an outside company.

The ballots utilized the voting system that Prince had set up, and which is still used to this day. It includes three spots, with first place receiving three points, two going to second place, and one to third.

"He wanted to do something that would take away from piling up the votes on just one guy, so he set up the voting system of 3-2-1," John Prince said of his father. "That really broke down a lot of favoritism in different parts of the country."

In that first year, Chicago's Berwanger received 84 total points, followed by Army's Monk Meyer (29), Notre Dame's William Shakespeare (23), and Princeton's Pepper Constable (20). Seeking to get the word out in an age where there was no national newspaper, Prince and his daughter went to Manhattan to the CBS Radio affiliate that transmitted *The Eddie Cantor Show* to ask if they'd announce the winner. Berwanger, though, would first receive a telegraph in late November informing him that he had won the upstart award, along with a trip for two to New York.

The Maroons halfback would be the only winner of the statue known as the Downtown Athletic Club Trophy, as less than a year after Berwanger's win, John Heisman died of bronchial pneumonia on October 3, 1936. Two months after his death, with the blessing of Heisman's widow, Edith Maora Heisman, the award was renamed in her husband's honor. Every year until her death in '64, the DAC sent Edith Heisman flowers the week of the announcement.

In the decades that would follow, as names like Niles Kinnick, Doak Walker, and Paul Hornung joined its fraternity, Heisman the trophy had in the minds of many come to overshadow Heisman the man.

"The award is wonderful," Mike Garrett said upon his 1965 win, "but who's Heisman?"

It's now a spectacle, a primetime TV event with a votership that had ballooned to over 1,300 before being trimmed down, and as of 2016 sits at 930 with the addition of its most recent winner, Alabama running back Derrick Henry. The Downtown Athletic Club went bankrupt in 2002, largely due to the September 11 terrorist attacks in New York that damaged the facility, and now the Heisman Trust, with a number of corporate sponsors behind it, administers the award.

But those humble beginnings, from a publicity push that was the idea of a journal editor and a hunk of bronze crafted by an impoverished artist, still matter and are still its backbone.

They are especially important to those whose family and whose hands brought it into existence.

John Prince and his wife were on vacation in Sarasota, Florida, in 1977 to see the Ringling Museum of Art and Sallie picked up a local newspaper that included an article on the sculptor who had created two bronze busts of John and Mable Ringling.

"Hey," Sallie said. "There's a picture of someone down here who they say sculpted the Heisman Trophy."

"Well, if his name isn't Frank Eliscu," John said, "he's lying."

"That is his name," Sallie answered.

"You're kidding," John replied, stunned.

Prince tracked down Eliscu and the two became close. When the sculptor died in 1996, the DAC reached out to Prince to write an article for its journal about his passing. Alongsde the article appeared a photo of the two with the original mold of the trophy.

For Prince, the Heisman has been a constant. Having helped to count those first ballots, he remains a collector of trophy memorabilia and has helped to raise hundreds of thousands for charity by selling signed balls that the Heisman Trust had supplied him.

But for Norma Eliscu Banas, the topic didn't truly come up until she was a teenager. When she was a young girl in Ossining, New York, she would often join her father in his studio in the garage in the backyard. He helped her create the likes of a ceramic cat and a pin adorned with copper enameling, items the now eighty-two-year-old retired educator still has.

"I used to go and try to learn how to do things and he was very patient," she said.

"He was dad. He was an accomplished artist." But over the years she'd learn, "It was something that you just said 'My dad did the Heisman Trophy,'" she said. "Wow. You got recognition."

That also comes every December when she sees a new winner claim the award, a yearly exhibit of her dad's work. It may not be "Cascade of Books," but decades later, Frank Eliscu's work is on display.

In that, Banas can't help but have two prevailing thoughts: one of a legacy formed, and the other of one later realized.

"That's my dad," she said. "It's tickling that people know who he is. . . . What's nice also is a lot of people do a one-time thing—when they're young, especially—but he did go and fulfill the promise of being something special and that's very nice."

That in itself is the story of this trophy, its winners, and the annual process of awarding it. Legends are made of youth, and the seeds of promise planted, but what is it that they do with the Heisman? Do they go on to NFL stardom? Do they flame out? Do they use it as a springboard to success in other walks of life?

The accomplishments of the four winners to go on to win Super Bowl MVPs—Staubach ('63), Jim Plunkett ('70), Marcus Allen ('81), and Desmond Howard ('91)—stand alongside those of Vic Janowicz ('50) and Bo Jackson ('85), the only recipients to play pro football and baseball, Charlie Ward ('93), who would spurn the NFL for the NBA, or war heroes Nile Kinnick ('39), Tom Harmon ('40), and Doc Blanchard ('45).

"It's truly an honor to be elected to this fraternity," said Reggie Bush, who won in 2005, but would return his trophy following a scandal at USC. "I've been in college for three years and it's the first time I've been invited into a fraternity."

They come together every December in New York, that football royalty, the few who have not just held that trophy, but understand that no other award in American sports carries the same cachet or expectations, no matter the endeavor.

"It kind of puts a lot of pressure on one guy," Barry Sanders said in his winning year of 1988.

But its recipients will forever carry this designation, one that makes them touchstones and idols for generations.

"You're known forever as a Heisman Trophy winner," said Tim Tebow ('07).

CHAPTER ONE
SHE USED IT AS A DOORSTOP

THE TROPHY THAT Jay Berwanger wanted shares shelf space in the archives room of the College Football Hall of Fame in downtown Atlanta, sitting nearby a portrait of Desmond Howard, a bust of Woody Hayes, and a plastic wig of Brian Bosworth's mid-1980s Mohawk/mullet (yes, they made Boz wigs).

The Silver Football, awarded by the *Chicago Tribune* to the Big Ten's Most Valuable Player (though, in those days it was deemed "the most useful player to his team"), was eleven years old when the Chicago Maroons running back entered his final season in 1935.

"The *Tribune* award made me happier at the time," Berwanger said fifty years later. "That was established, well known."

The Heisman Trophy wasn't. In fact, it wouldn't carry that name until its namesake, John Heisman, died months after Berwanger received the Downtown Athletic Club Trophy in 1935.

But while Berwanger's Silver Football has yet to see the exhibit floor in the HOF since it relocated from South Bend in 2014, his Heisman sits in the foyer of the Gerald Ratner Athletics Center—a $51 million, 150,000 square foot facility at the University of Chicago that opened in 2003. Encased in glass, it is displayed under the center of the rotunda, and expectedly, it has a tendency to steal attention.

Cuyler "Butch" Berwanger, Jay's youngest son, was on campus with friends when a group of prospective students and their parents entered the facility with a tour guide.

"She says, 'Here we are at the Ratner Center' . . . and before she can even say the word 'Heisman,' all these people walked past her and they went right up to it," Berwanger said. "[The tour guide] said, 'This happens every time.'"

For years, though, that trophy lived a life that was far less spectacular.

When Berwanger returned with the DAC award from New York, where he lugged around the trinket (unlike the modern-day version, which has a wooden base, the original sat atop black onyx marble, making it upwards of forty pounds), he had no clue what to do with it.

There was no suitable place for it in his small room in the Psi Upsilon house, and it became a nuisance as Berwanger attempted to study for exams. So he called his Aunt Gussie, who lived on the north side of the city, and asked her to keep it.

But Gussie didn't have a mantelpiece to display the hefty, stiff-armed award. She instead found a more practical use for it.

"She kept it in the hall on the floor and discovered it could be used as a doorstop," Berwanger said in 1990. "It was a very logical thing to do."

****

Even when Berwanger graduated and married his first wife, fellow Chicago alum Philomela Baker, in 1940, he still didn't reclaim his prizes.

The DAC trophy would serve in its capacity at Gussie's for fifteen years, and when Berwanger would visit "I'd toss my hat over it," he said.

Eventually, the award, along with the aforementioned Silver Football, newspaper clippings, and one of Berwanger's uniforms, were packed away and placed into a trunk that sat in her attic.

"Really, when we first moved to Hinsdale [Illinois] in 1950, there was nothing in the house that represented the fact that he won the Heisman Trophy or was All-American or captains of All-American teams or anything else," said Butch Berwanger.

It wasn't until a few years later that Butch, who estimates he was seven at the time, was even aware that his father had been the first winner of college football's most coveted award.

His brother, John Jay—who is three years older—came home from school and Butch heard him tell their mother, "One of the teachers had said 'Oh, Berwanger. Your dad won the Heisman Trophy.'"

"Who won the Heisman Trophy?" John asked.

"Well," their mother replied, "your dad won it."

He hadn't, to Butch's recollection, ever mentioned it before. Not once.

Even when the trunk made its way into the family's home, the DAC trophy was either in the basement or in the attic, never displayed ostentatiously.

"That was my dad," Butch said.

****

One of five children of an Iowa blacksmith and farmer, Berwanger's path seemed set. He would complete the industrial track at Dubuque High School, then become—more than likely—a mechanic or something of that nature. But his exploits in wrestling, track, and football changed that.

He competed at the state championships in track and wrestling, and in football he starred as a halfback, linebacker, punter, and kicker. In the final game of his high school career, Berwanger was responsible for all the scoring in Dubuque's 20–0 win, with three touchdown runs and two extra points.

Michigan came calling. So did Minnesota and Purdue, and in-state power Iowa. But Chicago never did.

Local businessman Ira Davenport would play a part in Berwanger landing with the Maroons, as did, inadvertently, Hawkeyes coach Burt Ingwersen.

Davenport, the owner of Dubuque Boat and Boiler Works (he was also a bronze medalist in the 800-meter run in the 1912 Olympics and former football coach at the city's Loras College), had hired Berwanger for a summer job. A product of the University of Chicago himself,

Davenport took Berwanger to the campus twice, where he met track coach Ned Merriam—another Olympian from the 1908 London Summer Games—and members of his future fraternity.

"Before I knew it, things fell into place and the university offered me a scholarship," Berwanger told the *Chicago Tribune* in '97. "I was seriously thinking about a career in business, and I thought I could make more contacts in Chicago, compared with a small town like Iowa City or Ann Arbor, Michigan. Plus, I was excited about the University of Chicago's academics."

He was also turned off by a speech that Ingwersen gave while speaking to Dubuque High School's football banquet during Berwanger's senior year in which he told the players they were traitors if they left the state of Iowa and went to another school.

"My dad just didn't like that," said Butch Berwanger. "He didn't like the pressure of having to go to an Iowa school because you were from Iowa."

Berwanger was given a full-tuition scholarship of $300, but he would still have to pay for his room and board, which forced him to work in the school's engineer department, cleaning the gymnasium, fixing toilets, and running elevators, to meet his financial needs.

"Times were tough then," he said in 1986.

He had expected to play for future Hall of Famer Amos Alonzo Stagg, who had been in charge of Maroons athletics for more than four decades. But during Berwanger's freshman year (at the time, first-year players weren't eligible to play at the varsity level), Stagg was forced to retire. He had turned seventy on August 16, 1932, and in October of that year, the school had invoked a rule that provided seventy was the age limit for members of the faculty.

In announcing the retirement of Stagg, who had a .617 winning percentage, seven Big Ten titles, two national titles, and eleven consensus All-Americans to his credit, Chicago's board of trustees said it had created a new job, chairman of the Committee on Intercollegiate Athletics, for the outgoing coach. Instead, Stagg left to take over at Pacific.

"I'm going west and feel like I'm twenty-one years old instead of seventy-one," Stagg would say. "I'm ready to start another career and am as happy as can be."

Athletic director T. Nelson Metcalf turned to Clark Shaughnessy, who had success at both Loyola of the South and Tulane. The brain behind the modern T-formation, though he would never use it at Chicago given his personnel, was lured by the chance to coach in the Big Ten.

He was hired as coach and physical education professor, which enabled him to receive lifetime tenure (since all Chicago professors received it) and a $7,500 annual salary. He also inherited a player in Berwanger, whom he would give number 99. "That was as close to a perfect 100 as I could get," Shaughnessy said.

****

Nicknamed Genius of the Gridiron, the One-Man Gang, and the Flying Dutchman (despite his German lineage), Berwanger was on the field as a halfback/receiver/defensive back/kicker for every play in Chicago's five conference games of his sophomore year.

A year later, in 1934, Berwanger was also playing quarterback and scored 8 touchdowns on 119 carries, completed 4 passes for 196 yards, had 186 yards on 18 punt returns, and totaled 3,026 yards on 77 punts. Against eventual co-national champion Minnesota, Berwanger had 14 tackles—in the first half.

"I have never met a finer boy or better football player than Jay Berwanger," Shaughnessy said. "You can say anything superlative about him and I'll double it."

Adding to the fact that at 6-foot, 195 pounds he often weighed more than any other player on the field, Berwanger wore a white single bar across his helmet. It was a necessity to protect a nose that had been broken in his final high school game and again during his freshman year, but it gave writers another nickname for him: "The Man in the Iron Mask."

"I was told if I broke it again, I wouldn't have any nose left to repair," Berwanger said years later.

During his junior year, Berwanger led Chicago to a 21–0 win over Indiana that had it, for the time being, atop the Big Ten standings. He had a 97-yard kickoff return for a touchdown and threw for a 40-yard score to John Baker, and the only points he wasn't responsible for were because of a safety that came after he had taken a seat on the bench in the third quarter.

Red Grange, the legendary Galloping Ghost, was on hand at Stagg Field that day in the press box. As the former NFL halfback told reporters, "[Berwanger] looks more like a real ghost to me, running through the rain and mud with that white mask on."

Five days later, the syndication service Newspaper Enterprise Association published a column by Grange in which he wrote, in part, about the attributes that make the perfect running back: a "faraway look" or field vision that allows a back to run at full speed, plant, and cut without altering pace; the power to run through the line; and constant speed. But within that speed, Grange explained, one needs an extra gear when required to slip outside when a hole closes or to pull away from tacklers.

The description, Grange admitted, was inspired by what he saw out of Berwanger vs. the Hoosiers. While the Hall of Famer added the caveat that even Berwanger wasn't all those things "[he] has a generous measure of those gifts."

In closing the piece, Grange wrote, "Jay Berwanger can play halfback on my team."

Berwanger did it all, basically, because he had to.

The Maroons were 3-3-2 overall and 0-3-2 in his sophomore season, finishing tied with Indiana for eighth in the Big Ten. Despite Berwanger's exploits as a junior, and helping Chicago to a 4–0 start and wins in its first two conference games, the team dropped its last four, including 33–0 at Ohio State and 35–7 vs. the Golden Gophers to end up seventh in the standings at 2–4.

That slide began with a 26–20 loss to Purdue in which Berwanger threw two scores, caught another, and had over 200 yards of offense.

But late in the game he suffered a bruised knee, and while the halfback made the trip to Columbus the following Saturday, Shaughnessy kept his star out as Chicago was outgained 266 to 130 and had half as many first downs as the Buckeyes' 14.

As the *Chicago Tribune*'s French Lane wrote that day, the Maroons appeared to be waiting for "somebody like Berwanger to come along and help them out of a desperate situation. Neither Berwanger nor anybody of any ability was forthcoming, so the Maroons did the best they could."

While Berwanger returned a week later against Minnesota, he wasn't enough against a powerhouse that had outscored its previous two opponents 64–0. Berwanger's double-digit tackle day, along with an interception that Barton Smith returned for a score, were among the few highlights in a game in which the Maroons managed 47 total yards.

He also handed out a souvenir to a Michigan defender who would someday be the most powerful man in the free world.

"When I tackled Jay one time, his heel hit my cheekbone and opened it up three inches," said Gerald R. Ford, the eventual thirty-eighth president of the United States.

Berwanger would recall a later run-in, saying, "When we met again, he turned his cheek and showed me a scar on the side of his face. He told me 'I got this trying to tackle you in the Chicago-Michigan game.'"

Berwanger wouldn't be a consensus All-American; that honor would go to Alabama's Dixie Howell, as Berwanger landed on the Associated Press second team, and received first-team nods via the All-American Board and Walter Camp Football Foundation.

"He is one of the finest players, one of the best defensive halfbacks I have ever seen," Shaughnessy said that season. "He can punt with the best in the country; he is a fine passer and a horse for work."

The coach took that final statement to heart during Berwanger's senior year, adding signal-calling responsibilities to his plate. A reluctance to call his own number resulted in Berwanger rushing 121 times that year, compared to 184 as a sophomore when he wasn't also serving as the quarterback.

But his average yards per carry had gone up each season, from 3.7 as a sophomore to 4.4 in his junior year and 4.8 as a senior, in totaling 577 yards. He had also improved as a passer, hitting on 26 of 68 attempts for 406 yards.

As the Maroons struggled again, going 4–4 and 2–3 in the Big Ten to tie Michigan for seventh in the standings, Berwanger's senior season would largely be remembered for his exploits in two games.

On November 9 he ripped off an 85-yard touchdown run which the AP writer on hand described as the Chicago star "dodging and twisting in the snakiest gallop seen on Stagg Field since the famed Red Grange."

Then, in the final game of his career, with the Maroons trailing Illinois 6–0, Berwanger took a punt at midfield in the third quarter and raced 49 yards before he was taken down from behind at the Illini 1-yard line.

On the next two plays, Berwanger called for fullback Warren Skoning, who was denied both times. Berwanger then plunged in for the touchdown himself before adding the extra point for what would be the decisive score. The *Tribune* headline after the win read "Berwanger 7, Illinois 6."

Berwanger would end his career with more than a mile of yardage from scrimmage, including 1,839 yards on the ground, 50 receptions, and 22 total touchdowns.

"There wasn't a man on the team who was jealous of Jay or who thinks he gets his just credit," Shaughnessy would later say. "They held him in affection and were proud to play on the same team."

A consensus All-American that season, as well as the recipient of the Silver Football he so sorely wanted, Berwanger also received a telegraph at his fraternity house from the Downtown Athletic Club telling him he'd been named the Outstanding College Football Player East of the Mississippi, beating Army's Monk Meyer by 55 points.

"I'd won a few things that year, and I might have ignored it if it didn't mention a plane trip to New York," Berwanger said. "I'd never been to New York, so I went. Had a real good time, too."

The biggest thrill, he would say many times, was his first trip on a plane as he and Shaughnessy attended a luncheon at the DAC in Berwanger's honor. Ellmore Patterson, the 1934 Chicago captain, and College Football Hall of Fame players Pa Corbin and Hector Cowan also attended.

"The best thing about Berwanger is that he's unspoiled by all this," Shaughnessy said. "He's a great kid as well as a natural athlete and good student."

Speculation around Berwanger's football future was a hot topic at the ceremony, but his playing days were over.

In another first, Berwanger was the No. 1 pick in the inaugural NFL draft in 1936 and was taken by the Philadelphia

The one and only winner of the Downtown Athletic Club Award, Chicago's Jay Berwanger beat Army's Monk Meyer by 55 points in 1935.
(Special Collections Research Center, University of Chicago Library)

Eagles. They offered him upwards of $150 a game, good money at the time given pro football's fledgling state, but Berwanger declined.

"'I thought I'd have a better future by using my education rather than my football skills," he would say.

His rights were traded to the Chicago Bears, and Berwanger set his demands knowing team owner-coach George Halas would never meet them. He asked for a two-year deal for $25,000 and a non-cut guarantee.

"We shook hands, said good-bye, and he and I have been good friends ever since," Berwanger said years later. "They just couldn't afford to pay that kind of money."

Berwanger's focus was on the Olympics, where he hoped to make the 1936 Berlin Games—which would be defined by Jesse Owens's exploits under the gaze of Adolf Hitler—but Chicago president Dr. Robert Hutchins had a disdain for sports. The man who scorned schools that received more attention for athletics than academics would abolish the football program in 1939. He also refused to extend scholarships, giving Berwanger the option to graduate or focus on Berlin.

"I couldn't try out for the Olympics and concentrate on my studies too," Berwanger said in 1997. "If I had gone to the Olympics, I might not have ever earned my degree. Besides, I was the president of my senior class and I felt I owed it to my classmates to stick around."

Berwanger instead graduated and took a $25-a-week job as a salesman with a Chicago rubber company. He would start Jay Berwanger Inc., a maker of plastic and sponge rubber strips for automobiles and farm machinery, after serving as an officer in the navy in World War II.

Football found a way of luring him back, as he became a coach with the Maroons months after graduating, leading the freshman team in 1936, and a year later, he added scouting duties.

He also spent fourteen years as a Big Ten official, and was at the center of controversy in the 1949 Rose Bowl between Northwestern and Cal.

During the second quarter, Wildcats fullback Art Murakowski fumbled as he lunged foward for a touchdown from one yard out. But referee Jimmy Cain signaled for a touchdown under the ruling that Murakowski's body crossed the plane before losing the ball and Northwestern would go up 13–7 en route to a 20–14 win.

Pictures disputing the play surfaced, and the heat fell on Berwanger, who was on the goal line outside of the defensive end.

"It appears to me that Cain shifted his own responsibility onto Berwanger," Jim Masker, the supervisor of Big Ten officials, said three days after the game. "It's up to the official in the best position to report his observations on a touchdown play, by nod or some other sign, but the decision on whether it is a score rests solely with the referee."

Of the dispute, Berwanger surmised, "It all depends on what part of the country you're from as to whether I called the play right."

But it's a scenario that seems almost unthinkable in today's game: an All-American running back making a call that ultimately helped his former conference win one of the most important games of the season.

Imagine Ricky Williams aiding the Big 12, Chris Weinke making a crucial call for the ACC, or Danny Wuerffel helping the SEC.

Regardless of intentions, it would be a circus.

"It doesn't make any sense," Butch Berwanger said. "You couldn't have gotten away with that now."

Jay Berwanger built his name away from the trophy, as a referee, yes, but primarily as a businessman. When he unloaded his company in the early 1990s, it was pulling in $30 million, and the Heisman was but a tool to create opportunities.

"He said that got you in the door because you could sign a picture for them or whatever, but that didn't get the client or keep the client," Butch said. "That just got you in the door."

That was the humility of Berwanger, but however much humility ruled his world, his legacy was in that standing as the oldest brother of the Heisman fraternity.

****

Berwanger and his second wife, Jane, were in New York for the Heisman ceremony in 1977, when Butch Berwanger walked in the back door of the couple's home to let their dogs out.

He turned on the little black-and-white television in the kitchen for white noise, walked into the bathroom, and when he returned, O. J. Simpson—the award's 1968 recipient—was on the screen, giving way to Jay Berwanger.

He took the stage amid a standing ovation and his son reached for the phone, calling his siblings. None of them were watching because their father told them there was no reason to do so.

"Thank you O. J.," he said, as he opened the envelope. "It is indeed a pleasure and an honor for me to be able to announce the 43rd Heisman winner and it goes to . . . Earl Campbell of the University of Texas."

When Butch picked up Jay and Jane at the airport, he wasted little time letting him have it.

"You are in big trouble," the son said. "When did you know that you were going to be on TV?"

"Oh, a couple days earlier," the father replied.

During a gathering before the ceremony, Simpson was discussing the plans for the announcement itself, which would come at the end of a variety show.

The initial plan was to have a celebrity announce the winner, but Simpson had another idea.

"That's Jay Berwanger, the first winner of the Heisman Trophy," Simpson said to co-host and actor Elliott Gould. "He's so admired by everybody. Have him open it."

In the award's first hour-long primetime event, which appeared on CBS (the network paid $200,000 for the rights), Gould and Simpson, both in tuxes, crooned "He's a Ladies' Man," a cringe-worthy moment given what history would have in store for a man who stood trial for the murder of his ex-wife. Connie Stevens and Leslie Uggams performed and Reggie Jackson and Paul Hornung—the 1956 winner—handed out the first DAC Awards.

Six players—UCLA's Jerry Robinson (linebacker), Chris Ward of Ohio State (offensive lineman), Notre Dame's Ken MacAfee (tight end), the Fighting Irish's Ross Browner (defensive lineman), Zac Henderson of Oklahoma (defensive back), and Campbell (running back)—were honored as the best at their position, a practice that was stopped after '78.

After the trophy was wheeled out onto the stage on a rolling column, Simpson stated, "Now to announce the winner of this year's Heisman, we have someone very special with us here tonight. The man who was the first recipient of the Heisman Trophy forty-three years ago . . . ladies and gentlemen, Mr. Jay Berwanger."

"He never thought, for two days, of calling us," Butch says, looking back. "[If I] was going to be on national television, [I] would tell somebody, and my dad didn't."

But the gesture by Simpson—beloved at the time—was indicative of the reverence the other Heisman winners had for Berwanger.

"I think we all just respected the heck out of Jay Berwanger, because he was the guy that got it started," said 1974 and '75 winner Archie Griffin. "Tremendous amount of respect whenever he was in the room. Everybody kind of just bowed down to him because of who he was and what he accomplished. Not just on the football field, but as a man."

Berwanger died in 2002 in his Oak Brook, Illinois, home after a long battle with lung cancer. He was eighty-eight.

For nearly sixty years, he would rarely miss a ceremony despite running his own company and often being on the road Monday through Friday. "He was really busy with all that," Butch said.

Yet after selling his company and enduring Jane's death in 1998, his place as the patriarch of the Heisman—that part of him that he never shunned, but was cavalier enough with it to leave his trophy with Aunt Gussie—moved to the forefront.

"I think he really enjoyed that kind of stuff then because that's what he had," Butch said. "That's what he had left."

In his late eighties, he again donned his number 99 uniform for a photo. He was still the Genius of the Gridiron, the One-Man Gang, the Flying Dutchman. As Griffin would recount, Berwanger was known to pull aside the winners to personally welcome them in. Jay Berwanger may have been more than twenty pounds lighter than the 195 he played at, but the uniform, and his role as the Heisman godfather, all fit.

"Later in life, [so many things] kind of faded away," Butch Berwanger said. "He really enjoyed the Heisman hype."

CHAPTER TWO

IDOL WORDS

THEY GATHERED AT Floyd Bennett Field on a balmy December day—at least, by Brooklyn, New York, standards—sitting on the runway outside of a US Navy plane that had just flown over Broadway. Navy officials and the Midshipmen's football captain, Al Bergner, were on board, but the contingent, led by Downtown Athletic Club director Bill Bradley was there for one reason, and it was written across the massive sign stretched out before them.

DOWNTOWN A.C. WELCOMES KINNICK 1939 HEISMAN FOOTBALL TROPHY WINNER.

Iowa's Nile Kinnick, the first megastar of the award's era, had arrived.

To be fair, more than a decade before Kinnick, Red Grange had captivated the nation at both the collegiate level at Illinois and in the professional ranks with the Chicago Bears and New York Yankees. In terms of Kinnick's contemporaries, Michigan's Tom Harmon was the one to appear on the covers of both *TIME* and *LIFE* magazines.

But it was what Kinnick represented in headlining an impossible turnaround for the Hawkeyes that captivated a nation.

"The city of New York and its 7,000,000 inhabitants, who rarely go overboard about anything, surrendered completely," wrote a *United Press* reporter about the Hawkeye halfback and his coach, Eddie Anderson, who, a day after Kinnick received his Heisman, was honored as Coach of the Year by the *New York World-Telegram*. Along with his plane ride over the city and a luncheon with navy officials, Kinnick received a kiss from Mary Jane Walsh, a Davenport, Iowa, native who was appearing on Broadway as Eileen Eilers in a run of *Too Many Girls*. The Mutual Broadcasting System was transmitting both *The Navy's Tribute to Nile Kinnick, Winner of the Heisman Trophy* and the award presentation ceremony.

"He has been in New York little more than 24 hours and already he has been presented with everything but the Statue of Liberty, the Empire State Building and the Trylon and Perisphere," wrote Jack Singer in the *New York Journal and American Sports*. "He expects someone to try and sell him the Brooklyn Bridge, but we so secretly suspect that he is smart enough to buy it and then sell it right back at a neat profit."

In 1938, Iowa had gone 1-6-1, but in 1939 a group that would be dubbed the "Ironmen" took down powers Notre Dame and Minnesota in consecutive weeks, allowing the team to finish 6-1-1. Kinnick played nearly every minute, including each play on offense, defense, and special teams over a five-game span.

Just 5-foot-8 and around 175 pounds, Kinnick ran for 374 yards and 5 touchdowns and hit on 31 passes for 638 yards and 11 scores. He delivered 16 of Iowa's 19 TDs and, with his kicking duties, was responsible for 107 of its 130 points.

"Nile was their leader," Dr. William Paul, the Hawkeyes' team doctor, told the *Daily Iowan* in 1972. "Nobody on the team was jealous of him. They depended on him and they followed him—and most of the time, Nile did not disappoint them."

Nor did he disappoint when addressing the press contingent at the Heisman dinner with a speech that, thanks to MBS, was broadcast across the nation.

After thanking his coach, teammates, the writers, and the Downtown Athletic Club, Kinnick said, "I would like, if I may, to make a comment which I think is appropriate at this time."

Coming two years before the United States began its involvement in World War II, he proclaimed his beliefs that the nation would be better served by staying out of the conflict.

Iowa's Nile Kinnick gave an impassioned speech in 1939, proclaiming his beliefs on whether the United States should be involved in World War II.
(Nile Kinnick Papers, University of Iowa Libraries, Iowa City, Iowa)

"I thank God that I was born to the gridirons of the Middle West and not to the battlefields of Europe. I can speak confidently and positively that the football players of this country would rather fight for the Heisman Trophy than for the Croix de Guerre."

At first, those in attendance remained silent.

The year before, TCU's Davey O'Brien was praised for the humbleness he exuded in a speech in which he said, "I am certainly appreciative of the high honor, but I feel I must give credit to the men who made me; to coach Dutch Meyer who taught me all I know, to his assistants, to those great linemen, Ki Aldrich and I. B. Hale . . . I am not much at speaking so cannot begin to tell you how much it all means. But I hope this will help."

The words of Yale's Clinton Frank, the 1937 recipient, the Associated Press reporter on hand penned, were "as calm and unaffected as the young man himself." The halfback closed out his acceptance by saying "Football has always been a sport, a game to me, and nothing more. I was interested in it as such, I played it as such, and I leave it as such."

Never before had a winner used the Downtown Athletic Club as a pulpit to deliver a message, and after that initial silence, the AP's Whitney Martin reported that "seven hundred men and women rose and cheered and whistled . . . You realized the ovation wasn't alone for Nile Kinnick, the outstanding college football player of the year. It was also for Nile Kinnick, typifying everything admirable in American youth."

****

Ironically, and tragically, Kinnick's fate would lie in that war from which he wished the US to absolve itself. After a year of law school in Iowa City, he enlisted in the Naval Air Reserve, writing, "There is no reason in the world why we shouldn't fight for the preservation of a chance to live freely, no reason why we shouldn't suffer to uphold that which we want to endure. May God give me the courage to do my duty and not falter."

He was called to active duty three days after Pearl Harbor and stationed in the Caribbean. On the morning of July 2, 1943, Kinnick's F4-F Wildcat developed an oil leak over the Gulf of Paria near Trinidad. The plane plunged into the sea, and while another pilot saw Kinnick bobbing in the water, by the time a rescue boat arrived, he was nowhere to be found. He was twenty-four years old.

"He was loved by everyone who knew him; his kindness and consideration for others stamped as a typically ideal American," Anderson said after word came from the navy that Kinnick had been killed in action. "In the uniform of his country he gave everything—that was the only way Nile Kinnick knew how to play the game."

Kinnick's legacy runs deep at Iowa, where the football stadium is named after him (he's the only Heisman winner to hold that honor) and a fourteen-foot-bronze statue of the halfback stands in front of the facility. But in terms of the Heisman as an institution, Kinnick's impact may have ultimately been in illustrating the potential of what the acceptance speech could be.

Kinnick set the precedent, and two years after his win, Minnesota's Bruce Smith would deliver his own iconic words as a nation tried to come to grips with one of its darkest moments.

The Golden Gophers star was on a train en route to the Heisman ceremony with his family on December 7, 1941, when news broke that 353 Imperial Japanese Navy planes, bombers, and torpedo planes had hit the U.S. naval base at Pearl Harbor. The attack claimed 2,403 Americans and left another 1,178 wounded.

With the help of his father, Lucius—a former Minnesota tackle—Bruce Smith (the winner of an especially tight race—554 votes to 345 for Notre Dame's Angelo Bertelli, making it the narrowest margin in the trophy's short history) went to rewriting his speech while they made their way to NYC. He tried to find the proper way to accept an award when sports couldn't seem much less important.

If there was any doubt as to the mood and the tensions the nation was dealing with, an anxious moment came as Smith stepped forward to accept the trophy, as a squadron of army planes had been mistaken for German bombers and an air raid alert was signaled along the East Coast.

"So much of emotional significance has happened in such a brief space of time," Smith began his speech, delivered one day after the US had declared war, "that the task of responding on such an occasion leaves me at a loss to assign relative value."

He spoke of adding his name to a list that began with Berwanger and, the year before, welcomed Michigan's Tom Harmon, and of the gratitude and appreciation he felt. Smith thanked his coach, Bernie Bierman, and his teammates, before turning his attention to the tragic attack in Hawaii that would usher in the United States' arrival in the conflict.

"In the Far East they may think American boys are soft, but I have had, and even have now, plenty of evidence in black and blue to prove that they are making a big mistake. I think America will owe a great debt to the game of football when we finish this thing off. If six million American youngsters like myself are able to take it and come back for more, both from a physical standpoint and that of morale. If teaching team play and cooperation and exercise to go out and fight hard for the honor of our schools, then likewise the same skills can be depended on when we have to fight to defend for our country."

It was more than just a rally for the nation, as Smith—like Kinnick and Harmon—became a fighter pilot, though he wouldn't see combat and played service football for the Great Lake Navy team.

A year after his Heisman victory, he played himself in an autobiographical movie *Smith of Minnesota*. "See this triple-threat bolt of greased lightning hit a new high for red-blooded entertainment!" a tagline on the original poster promised, but as his wife, Gloria, would tell ESPN. com, "If they took the word 'swell' out of the script, it would be a silent movie." Nonetheless, after Smith's death in 1967 at age forty-seven after a long bout with cancer, a Paulist priest, Rev. William Cantwell, proposed Smith for sainthood in the Roman Catholic Church. The priest told the National Catholic News Service he had invoked the intercession of Smith many times on behalf of cancer patients.

Kinnick and Smith provided a measure of the strength of a nation's Golden Boys in a time when the opportunities to speak to such a vast audience were rare. They delivered words that met the moment, words both profound and galvanizing.

It's something that 2001 Heisman recipient Eric Crouch has thought about over the years.

Three months removed from the September 11 terrorist attacks, the ceremony had to be moved to the Marriott Marquis Hotel in Times Square due to damage suffered by the DAC, which stood blocks from Ground Zero. Eleven DAC members had died in the attacks on the World Trade Center.

As Crouch took the podium, he said, "A long time ago, I never thought I could do something like this, but I always believed in myself. Deep down inside you want that trophy, but win or lose I always want to be the same person—keeping my character and keeping composed." But he made no mention of the attacks or the uneasiness felt across the country despite 9/11 weighing heavily over the proceedings.

"Maybe it was something that I missed, because if I missed it—which I did, clearly miss it on that stage—it's something that I think about a lot," Crouch said in 2016. "Not that I missed it, but [because] of what was happening time-wise, with the United States and that huge event.

"I think part of it was just maybe not thinking that was an opportunity for me to say something, I guess I want to say, almost politically. I think I have more of an opinion about it now than I did when I was twenty-three. If I had to do it again, I would have definitely mentioned it. There's no doubt about. It affected me greatly, because I never got to experience the Downtown Athletic Club. That was the first year, because of 9/11."

For decades, winners had the benefit of time, learning they were the Heisman recipient before even heading to New York, and could craft their speeches as such, unlike today's players, who find out at the end of America's longest-running reality show. As Wisconsin's Alan Ameche, the 1954 winner, described the growth in an interview conducted in '82: "There were maybe ninety or a hundred people in the room. Because the space was so limited, some of my relatives couldn't get in . . . I come back almost every year and it boggles my mind to see the difference. They have a big dinner at the Hilton Hotel with two to three thousand people."

The drama of a made-for-TV-moment has largely replaced thoughtfulness with spontaneity, the culmination of months of hype thrust upon a player who is asked to go before a massive audience and have his say. It's no different than any other award show, but most other award shows aren't centered around college students.

But there's also the growth of sports and media at the center of what later players would feel was their responsibility. Kinnick and Smith spoke at a time when college football players were among the US's biggest stars—it still dwarfed the pro game in popularity and at times overshadowed the whole of sport, with Kinnick beating out the Yankees' Joe DiMaggio and boxer Joe Louis for the 1939 AP Athlete of the Year. To them, the Downtown Athletic Club presented a rare opportunity to speak on a national stage, something modern winners have on an almost daily basis.

The speeches that followed Kinnick's and Smith's weren't legendary moments with messages either political or patriotic. They, instead, delivered raw emotion.

"I wish I would have had more prepared," Crouch said. "I really didn't expect to walk away with the Heisman Trophy that night. It's exhausting, because you're on national television, cameras in front of you. It's your opportunity and I remember the one thing I forgot to do is I was thanking everybody else but my team. Mentors and coaches and my girlfriend at the time—[who] is my wife now—parents. You thank everybody and you're up there and I just happen to forget to thank my teammates."

As Derrick Henry told reporters the day before he won in 2015: "It's nerve-racking. But at the same time, we're here to talk about what got you to this moment and who you're thankful for. So I don't think it'll be that hard speaking from the heart. I wrote some stuff down. If it happens, I'll speak from the heart."

Henry did just that in an eight-minute, seventeen-second address. "I'm a little nervous. I don't do this every day," he began. The Crimson Tide star gave his thanks to those who had impacted him, but he struck a nerve when he closed by recognizing former teammate Altee Tenpenny, who had died in a one-car accident October 20, 2015. Henry had posted a message on Instagram after Tenpenny's death, writing, "I will continue to keep your name alive & you always live through me & I hope I can keep dancing & smiling as I continue my journey while you watch over me."

"Rest in peace, my brother Altee Tenpenny, he's been a brother to me, who died this year," Henry told a nation that night in New York. "I just want to tell him I love him and I miss him."

Henry's emotional tribute was not the first—nor will it likely be the last—delivered within the spotlight of the Heisman speech. John Cappelletti and Mark Ingram were among those who provided heart-rending moments that have often overshadowed what they did on the field.

****

Cappelletti, the Penn State running back, ushered in the dominance of his position in the history of the award, as the first of 11 straight victories by running backs, but his yardage in his winning season of 1973—1,522—was well below the 1,843 those runners after him averaged, and during that period, only Ohio State's Archie Griffin had less with 1,450 in his repeat year of '75. Cappelletti won handedly, though, coming in 533 points ahead of Ohio State offensive tackle John Hicks, while Texas's Roosevelt Leaks—the closest running back—was in third, 575 points behind the Nittany Lion.

Likewise, Ingram was the workhorse of Alabama's 2009 title team and the first trophy recipient in that program's long, storied history. His win, though, was almost an aberration for a running back among an era dominated by quarterbacks putting up monster numbers, as the vacating of Reggie Bush's '05 trophy leaves him as the only running back in a fourteen-year span to claim the Heisman.

Neither player led the nation in rushing those seasons, either, but they are linked in another way in how they addressed the nation as a Heisman winner.

Penn State's John Cappelletti was among those who had the benefit of knowing he'd already won when he stood in front of a packed New York Hilton ballroom, and what was more stunning was that what unfolded wasn't scripted.

Nittany Lions co-captain Mark Markovich was rooming with Cappelletti that weekend, and he recounted to *USA TODAY* in 2003 that the running back had left a note card on the nightstand next to his bed and Markovich couldn't help but peek.

"The card said, 'To my coaches, to family and friends and someone special.' I said to John, 'What is this?' He grabbed it from my hand and said, 'You'll find out.'"

That was it. Yet, as Cappelletti looked out into the crowd that included his eleven-year-old brother, he managed to turn the night and the award into a symbol of the human spirit.

His voice quivered as he spoke to the crowd, which included Vice President Gerald Ford, sitting next to him on the dais.

"The youngest member of my family, Joseph, is very ill. He has leukemia. If I can dedicate this trophy to him tonight and give him a couple days of happiness, this is worth everything . . ."

The Cappellettis first learned that Joey had leukemia when he was five years old, and the child entered Philadelphia Children's Hospital for treatment with forty-six others afflicted with leukemia. Joey, at that time, was the only one still alive. He had to endure bone marrow tests and, in 1972, had slipped into a coma for a week.

Big brother John had to wipe away tears with a napkin as he continued.

"I think a lot of people think that I go through a lot on Saturdays and during the week as most athletes do, and you get your bumps and bruises and it is a terrific battle out there on the field. Only for me, it is on Saturdays and it's only in the fall. For Joseph, it is all year-round and it is a battle that is unending with him and he puts up with much more than I'll ever put up with and I think that this trophy is more his than mine because he has been a great inspiration to me."

Archbishop Fulton J. Sheen, asked to give the traditional blessing at the conclusion of the trophy presentation dinner, said, "Maybe for the first time you have heard a speech from the heart and not from the lips. Part of John's triumph was made by Joseph's sorrow. You don't need a blessing. God has already blessed you in John Cappelletti."

Chemotherapy would drive Joey's illness into remission, allowing him to play Little League baseball, but on April 8, 1976, he lost his eight-year battle, dying at his home in suburban Philadelphia. His brother John was at his bedside.

"We never gave up hope that he would live, but we always knew it was just a matter of time," Joey's father, John Sr., said at the time. "John can't speak. He is very emotional about this."

Watching Cappelletti's speech, Jerry McNeely wept, but the writer-producer was also struck with an idea. A month after Joey's death, he approached John about creating what became *Something for Joey*, a made-for-TV movie about the boy's life and death starring Marc Singer as John Jr., Jeffrey Lynas as Joey, and Paul Picerni in the role of Joe Paterno, who was unavailable due to preparations for the '77 Gator Bowl. Along the way, the family allowed him to spend a couple of weeks with them, and he also worked with Penn State. The film was nominated for a Golden Globe for Best Motion Picture Made for Television and two Primetime Emmy Awards for top director Lou Antonio; McNeely was up for best original teleplay.

"I just want people to see it," Cappelletti told the *Los Angeles Times* the night of its premier, "because I think there's a message here for everyone. It was my parents' decision to let Jerry McNeely go ahead and make it. They decided it would do more good than if nothing at all were made. It's a touchy situation. But we've seen it and we feel everything was portrayed pretty close to what actually happened."

It was turned into a book of the same name and published in 1983, and years later, the message of strength and courage that Cappelletti relayed continues to resonate.

"I get a lot of mail from kids who have brothers and sisters who aren't all that kind to each other sometimes. After they read the book, they're determined to change that stuff," Cappelletti told *USA TODAY*. "It's having an impact on a whole other generation, it seems like. Time doesn't seem to change that."

Cappelletti's heartache was largely unknown when he took the stage, but the same can't be said for Ingram when he won in 2009.

The Alabama running back took a deep breath after he was announced as the winner over Stanford's Toby Gerhart in the closest vote ever—a mere 28 points. The legends behind him on the stage encouraged him to "Take your time. . . . Take your time. . . . It's all right."

"I'm a little overwhelmed right now," Ingram said. "I'm sorry."

He dabbed his eyes. A few miles away from what was then known as Best Buy Theater, Ingram's father, Mark Sr., was watching in a New York holding facility.

Less than a year before his son won the Heisman, the senior Ingram was arrested in a Flint, Michigan, hotel room on January 2, 2009 where he was preparing to watch his son and the Crimson Tide play in the Sugar Bowl against Utah. Out on $200,000 bail after pleading guilty to money laundering and bank fraud, he had been granted a delay to watch his son play his freshman season at Alabama, then asked for another to see the Tide in the Southeastern Conference Championship Game on December 6, the day after he was supposed to report. The judge refused and Ingram fled to Michigan, failing to surrender to the federal prison in Kentucky to begin a seven-year, eight-month term.

"When it came to the eleventh hour, I had to make a decision," Ingram Sr. told *USA TODAY* in 2009. "My decision was to be with my son in what would be my last chance to watch him play in person in college."

An additional twenty-seven months would be added to his sentence the following March, but the father was still awaiting sentencing the night of the ceremony and watched on TV with fifteen other inmates who were also in limbo.

This was the reality Ingram Jr. lived with as he stood there, and let the emotions wash over him.

"I'd like to thank my family," the running back said through tears, motioning to them in the crowd. "My mother and my grandparents are sitting right there. My father, who has been a great influence on my life and I love him to death."

The following year, the absence of the winner's father again became the focus. Auburn's Cam Newton pointed a massive spotlight on the awkwardness of what should have been a coronation for the dynamic quarterback.

"I'd like to thank my beautiful mother, Jackie," he said. "And my father. You know this . . ." Newton stopped, put his head down, and appeared to be fighting back tears.

What would he say? What could he say?

Cecil Newton wasn't in the crowd. He had released a statement earlier that week saying, in part, "I have decided not to be in attendance . . . as it will perhaps rob Cam and the event of a sacred moment."

Nonetheless, the elder Newton's presence was unavoidable, with the specter of an NCAA investigation into a pay-for-play scheme with Mississippi State and the fact that Auburn had limited his access after the governing body declared the father had broken rules.

Despite a truly transcendent performance on the field, as the 6-foot-6, 250-pound junior threw for 2,589 yards and ran for 1,409 in totaling 49 touchdowns and a nation's-best 188.1 pass efficiency rating, the Football Writers Association of America (FWAA) made his son pay, omitting him from the All-American team and now, the dark cloud prompted 105 voters to leave him off their ballots.

Would Newton come to his father's defense? Would he address the scandal?

The quarterback stood there, trying to collect himself, and Bo Jackson, Auburn's 1985 winner, told Newton, "Take a couple deep breaths, man. Take a couple deep breaths."

"Thank you," Newton said, composing himself. "Thank you."

"WE LOVE YOU, CAM!" someone from the crowd yelled.

Newton flashed that smile, that thousand-watt grin that would soon be on commercials and seen while he was dabbing and dancing his way to the NFL's 2015 MVP award for the Carolina Panthers, then continued, "My parents do a lot of things behind the scenes that go unnoticed."

It was these words that would draw the most fire. Given his insistence that he knew nothing of the money his father was alleged to have wanted from the Bulldogs, Newton pointing to what his parents did behind the scenes drew criticism from those who watched the scandal unfold, and to include it in his speech seemed tone deaf on his part. Regardless, it shone a brighter light on the cloud that hung over the vote, none of it befitting of just how dominant his season was as the third player in FBS history to have 20 rushing touchdowns and 20 passing in the same season, following Tim Tebow and Colin Kaepernick.

"This is not an award, in my opinion, that has been won with my play this year," Newton went on. "This is an award that has been won ever since I came out of your womb. Thank you for everything you do for me and my family—and to my father, I love you so much."

With controversy swirling, it was what Newton could or couldn't—depending on what you believed—say that created the most interest around his win.

Just a year later, Robert Griffin III managed to do something impressive in its own right: make a statement before he'd said a single word of his speech.

As the Baylor quarterback was announced as the seventy-seventh Heisman winner, he flashed Superman socks for ESPN's cameras, then bowed his head and broke into a wide smile.

"Well, now that my socks are out there, I have nothing to lose," Griffin said as he let out a sigh at the podium.

The socks, which were blue with the iconic "S" logo at the top, included a cape that hung down from his calf near the ankle. Griffin wearing them spiked sales, with pairs going for as much as $500 on eBay in the days after the quarterback's unveiling. The Superman museum in the character's "official" hometown of Metropolis, Illinois, sold out, but accepted preorders for "the reasonable price of $18.95 a pair."

Those were apparently just a taste of what's in his arsenal, as Griffin disclosed that his sock collection also includes—but is not limited to—Angry Birds, Cookie Monster, Elmo, Scooby Doo, and his favorite pair, SpongeBob SquarePants. Said the quarterback in his news conference after the ceremony, as he showed off his Superman socks again, "If I can get everybody in the crowd to laugh it can make my speech a whole lot easier."

RG3's speech didn't offer the power of Kinnick and Smith or the emotion of Cappelletti and Ingram. Nor did it offer the intrigue of Newton. But Griffin's Heisman speech served as a platform for setting a fashion trend.

That showed a true evolution.

CHAPTER THREE

A VOTE DRIVEN
BY FOUR BIASES

A **BALLOT COULDN'T GET** much more simplistic, yet at the same time stand as a bigger lightning rod for criticism.

Unlike the Maxwell Award, Chuck Bednarik Award, Biletnikoff Award, Davey O'Brien Award, or any of college football's other major prizes, which submit preseason watch lists and narrow contenders down to three finalists, the Heisman Trophy is truly an exercise in individual liberties.

The form includes three blank lines with just one disclaimer:

In order that there will be no misunderstanding regarding the eligibility of a candidate, the recipient of the award MUST be a bona fide student of an accredited college or university including the United States Academies. The recipient must be in compliance with the bylaws defining an NCAA Student-Athlete.

That's it. Being in good standing with the NCAA is the only stated guideline placed before the hundreds of voters—in full disclosure, the author has been part of that contingent since 2008—creating a blank slate that would make it seem as if anyone from anywhere could win.

But that hasn't always been the reality.

Unwritten rules based largely on the four predominant biases: a player's position, class, school, and region (and for decades, the color of their skin) can exclude candidates no matter how impressive their numbers are, and set the short list of perceived favorites long before the season even starts.

Some of those limitations can and have been overcome—most notably, in recent years, the ageism of denying underclassmen—but for much of the award's history, ceilings were constructed from biases. Neither a strictly defensive player nor any true freshman has ever won and those from outside the sport's power conferences aren't often viewed as legitimate contenders, with just two such recipients having been recorded thus far. It's not meant to be a career achievement award, but there have been instances in which it has been voted on as such.

"It sure is a prestigious, highly visible award for there to be so much ambiguous criteria," said Archie Manning in a 1997 interview. In 1970, he finished third in a race won by Jim Plunkett.

So how can we be sure the player who hoists that fabled trophy in Times Square every December truly is, as the Heisman Trust's mission statement reads, "the outstanding college football player whose performance best exhibits the pursuit of excellence with integrity?"

We can't.

That mere fact makes the prospect of following the annual race to New York City for the ceremony—and the responsibility of voting for it—both fascinating and maddening. Yes, at its core, we're talking about something as inane as a college student being given a trophy, but the arguments and controversy this particular award elicits make it so captivating.

Some have argued the electorate is too large or that some of those who are a part of it don't see enough games or are swayed by the media pushes behind players from the major conferences. They're all valid points and, while a move to a selection committee à la the other top awards could help to educate voters and strip away some of the favoritism, it would also rob the Heisman of what makes it unlike any other award in sports.

Outstanding is truly subjective. But through the years the pursuit of defining it from season to season has shown us (though it has bent in some regards) that it can also be painstakingly exclusive.

Race isn't the issue it once was before Syracuse's Ernie Davis won in 1961 as the first black Heisman winner; in hindsight, it was arguably a sticking point in the 1956 vote when Paul Hornung took the trophy on a 2–8 Notre Dame team (he remains the only winner on a losing team) over the Orange's dominant Jim Brown. Houston's Andre Ware also broke through for black quarterbacks in '89, leaving four distinct biases that hang over voting.

Andre Ware became the first recipient from a team that was barred from playing on TV when the Houston quarterback won in 1989.
(By University of Houston, Courtesy of Special Collections, University of Houston Libraries.)

Bias No. 1: Region

While the ballot itself remains the same as the one that Willard B. Prince developed in 1935, voting since 1977 has consisted of six regions that include 145 media votes each, giving us 870 of the 930 votes (the rest consists of former winners, as well as a single fan vote). The regions are as follows:

- Far West: Arizona, California, Hawaii, Idaho, Montana, North Dakota, Nevada, Oregon, South Dakota, Utah, Washington, Wyoming
- Mid-Atlantic: Delaware, District of Columbia, Maryland, North Carolina, New Jersey, Pennsylvania, South Carolina, Virginia, West Virginia

- Midwest: Iowa, Illinois, Indiana, Michigan, Minnesota, Ohio, Wisconsin
- Northeast: Connecticut, Maine, Massachusetts, New Hampshire, New York City, New York (state), Rhode Island, Vermont
- South: Alabama, Florida, Georgia, Kentucky, Louisiana, Mississippi, Tennessee
- Southwest: Arkansas, Colorado, Kansas, Missouri, Nebraska, New Mexico, Oklahoma, Texas

The voting numbers that determine the winner, and those that since the practice began in 1982, are used to select the finalists who will attend the ceremony—a figure that is set by the natural break in the tallies, which is why we've seen as many as six players reach New York (1994 and 2013) and as few as three (ten times)—come from the overall point totals. But those aforementioned regions, and how a player performs in them in their home sector as opposed to the rest of the nation, can provide us a road map as to how someone won, or didn't win, the trophy.

That is the foundation for one of the most oft-discussed points in the Heisman balloting: East Coast Bias.

Joey Harrington knows it all too well. Oregon ended the 2000 season with a school-record 10 wins and ranked seventh in the Associated Press Top 25, the Ducks' highest finish ever. They achieved this success with the help of the redshirt junior quarterback, who had thrown for 2,967 yards and 22 touchdowns.

That season, Harrington helped put the Ducks back on the map, as ESPN's GameDay descended upon Eugene, marking the first time it had ever been to the Northwest. It was just the show's second time on the West Coast, coming in 1998 at UCLA.

"We were not the flashy Oregon team that is changing uniforms every week and little kids want to emulate," Harrington said. "We were a bunch of nobodies that kind of made a splash and were trying to get a foothold in college football, so people weren't exactly seeking out our games on Saturdays."

The school made a $250,000 gamble to make sure they did, using funds from boosters for a 10-story billboard of the quarterback in Times Square that dubbed him "Joey Heisman."

In his senior season, Harrington would throw for 2,764 yards and 27 touchdowns as well as six interceptions, including one that led to a 49–42 loss to Stanford at Autzen Stadium that ultimately kept the Ducks from playing for a national title.

It didn't help matters that he struggled in his final regular-season game against Oregon State, completing 11 of 22 passes for 104 yards and no scores in a 17–14 win, and it didn't aid his cause that he had a lack of national TV exposure.

Harrington would be the Pac-10 Offensive Player of the Year and earn second-team All-American honors, but it wasn't enough to claim the Heisman.

That went to Nebraska's Eric Crouch (770 points), with Florida's Rex Grossman (708) and Miami's Ken Dorsey (638) close behind, while Harrington (364) was a distant fourth in what, at the time, was the fourth-tightest race in the award's history.

Harrington won the Far West, earning 137 of his points, but he finished no higher than fourth in any other region.

Complicating matters, just 585 of the 922 ballots were returned, with the 63.3 return rate the lowest since 53 percent (541 of 1,050) came in during the 1978 voting, when Billy Sims won. The September 11 terrorist attacks, which disrupted mail service, played its part in the low return rate, which was well below the 80 percent average at the time.

Harrington was a finalist, the first in school history, but even now he can't help but feel like the uniform he was wearing played its part in the finish.

"I absolutely felt like if I was playing at Nebraska or Michigan or Ohio State or Texas, I definitely think people would have paid more attention," Harrington said.

That was underscored following a 38–16 drubbing of Colorado in the Fiesta Bowl, a performance in which the Ducks quarterback threw for 350 yards and 4 touchdowns to help Oregon finish second in the AP poll.

"The thing that always struck me was, I had more people come up to me after the Fiesta Bowl and say 'I wish I would have voted for you,'" Harrington said. "In the Fiesta Bowl we were on national television, prime time, and everybody could see it."

"Granted, I played one of my better games that day and it coincided with Eric Crouch struggling [114 yards rushing as the Cornhuskers were held to a season-low 239 in total] against [an] incredible Miami team. But that's what struck me more than anything is, that not that people didn't turn in their ballots, but people didn't look that closely or didn't have the ability or the time and once they did see it and see the product that we put out, it was kind of an awakening."

The following year, USC's Carson Palmer won the Heisman, followed by Jason White (Oklahoma) and the Trojans' Matt Leinart and Reggie Bush (though the latter was later vacated) in 2004 and '05, giving the Far West three winners in a four-year span, as many as it had in the previous twenty-one. But it wouldn't be until Oregon's Marcus Mariota swept all six regions in a 2014 victory that the Far West produced its first non-USC recipient from a power conference since Stanford's Plunkett in 1970.

"I think for a little while there, things changed in that, you saw that the next year, Carson Palmer won the Heisman . . . I think that a few more people were paying attention," Harrington said.

The Far West went through an impressive stretch from 1962–70, with its first winner, Oregon State's Terry Baker, setting off a run followed by USC's Mike Garrett (1965), UCLA's Gary Beban ('67), USC's O. J. Simpson ('68), and Plunkett. But those first two victories, and the years that came before them, showed the disconnect the contenders had with some voters in other parts of the country.

In the first seventeen years after the pool of candidates expanded past the Mississippi River in 1936, no one from the Far West had finished higher than Stanford's Frankie Albert and UCLA's Paul Cameron, who were both third in 1941 and '53, respectively.

Albert barely registered outside his home sector, winning there and coming in second in the Midwest, but he didn't make another top five. It was the start of a trend, as four others—UCLA's Donn Moomaw ('52), Cal's Paul Larson ('54), Stanford's John Brodie ('56), and Cal's Joe Kapp ('58)—all won the Far West, but couldn't mount a serious challenge elsewhere. Only Moomaw—fourth in the East and Southwest—made the top five in another region out of that group.

It made it all the more surprising then, when Baker showed a reach that went outside the Pacific Northwest in 1962, when he added a first place in the East to go with his Far West win. Baker's outing that October against previously unbeaten West Virginia in Portland, when Baker tossed three first-half touchdowns in a 51–22 rout, certainly helped his cause.

He was third in the Southeast and fourth in the Midwest, though he didn't even make the South's top five.

"I was hoping, like every other football player in America does, but I certainly didn't expect it," Baker said days after the announcement. "I knew they'd never given it to a West Coast player before and I had some concern."

Three years later, the Trojans' Garrett failed to take the Midwest (second) or Southwest (fourth), despite winning the Far West, South, and East. Beban claimed those same regions in '67, along with the Southwest, and was runner-up in the Midwest. Simpson would become the first from the region to claim all five voting sectors, a feat that Plunkett would accomplish two years later.

Those victories could have signaled that the Far West had turned the corner, and while that was true to a degree, it wound up being true for USC more than anyone.

Between Plunkett's win and that of BYU's Ty Detmer in 1990, the Trojans had a virtual stranglehold on the region, adding wins from Charles White ('79) and Marcus Allen ('81), along with second-places via Anthony Davis ('74), Ricky Bell ('76), and Rodney Peete ('88). In that twenty-one-year span, only three schools in the Far West region had anyone finish higher than third—Cal with Chuck Muncie in '75, Stanford's John Elway ('82), and BYU's Steve Young ('83).

Maybe that had something to do with the phone call the Downtown Athletic Club received from Elway's father, Jack, after sending a note inviting the Cardinal quarterback to the ceremony.

"Unless his son was going to win he was not going to come," recalled then-DAC athletic director Rudy Riska. "He felt he was not there to hype the Heisman, which in all the history of it, nobody ever turned us down."

Elway attended, finishing 695 points behind Herschel Walker, and it would be the start of an odd relationship for Stanford and the award's voting. The Cardinal would also have a player come in second four more times, including three straight in Toby Gerhart ('09) and Andrew Luck ('10 and '11) and, most recently, Christian McCaffrey ('15).

Gerhart had led the nation in rushing (1,736 yards at the time of voting), but lost the trophy by the smallest margin in history at 28 points. Six years later, McCaffrey broke Barry Sanders's single-season all-purpose yardage record with 3,496 by the regular season's end. But both lost to Alabama running backs—Mark Ingram and Derrick Henry, respectively—who played a major role in the Crimson Tide getting a shot at, and eventually claiming, national championships.

The fact that its teams often play games that don't kick off until 10 p.m. ET always played against the Far West teams, and specifically the Pac-12. While that's a gap that Harrington believes was narrowed for a time, advances in technology that should make for more informed voters may instead be responsible for them tuning out.

"[Contenders] were out there and [voters] were paying attention," Harrington said, "and I think once everything because instantly accessible—you can watch just about anything you want on your phone now—people have kind of gotten lazy and fallen back into that 'Well, I'll just check the highlights tomorrow.'"

At first glance, Mariota's win and McCaffrey finishing second in consecutive seasons may say otherwise, but consider that in this latest vote, McCaffrey won the Far West and finished second in the other five regions, though he had just six second-place votes more than third-place finisher Deshaun Watson of Clemson (246 to 240). It didn't help matters that seven of Stanford's games started after 10 p.m. ET or later.

The Far West hasn't been alone in feeling the lack of support from other regions, specifically when it comes to battling the challenges of games played in different time zones. Five times, the Southwest—in 1939, 1941, 1945, 1954, and 1962—saw a player win its vote but fail to make another top five. But its first trophy recipient, TCU's Davey O'Brien, came twenty-four years before Baker broke through for the West Coast, and since 1980, the Southwest has ten winners to the five recognized victors out of the Far West.

"I'm sure there is a little bit of a bias, because it's real hard for people in the East to see all the West Coast games," Palmer said in 2002. "Hopefully, the West Coast guys will stick behind their man."

More than a decade after Palmer made that statement, McCaffrey is proof that there's still more than a little truth in that sentiment. Where a player resides, though, can and has been overcome time and again in a Heisman race.

What position he plays, and more to the point, which side of the ball he plays on, makes for a different story entirely.

Bias No. 2: Position

Heading into the 1980 season, Pittsburgh's Hugh Green was a two-time All-American and after just his sophomore season, had been named to the Panthers' all-time team. If he were a quarterback or a running back, everyone else would have been chasing him. But Green was a defensive end, and as dominant as he was up to that point in his career, racking up 337 tackles and 36 sacks in his first three years, there was an inescapable truth.

"It's going to go to a kid who is explosive, who can win a game," Pitt's defensive coordinator Foge Fazio told the *Pittsburgh Post-Gazette* prior to the 1980 season. "I think, being realistic, it's a fact of life that the Heisman will go to an offensive player."

Green would be the first defender to claim United Press International Player of the Year, and also won the Walter Camp Award, the Maxwell Award, and the Lombardi, and once again, he was a first-team All-American as the 6-foot-2, 222-pounder had 123 tackles (including 11 for loss) and 17 sacks.

"Hugh has been the best defensive player in the country the past three years in my opinion," Pitt coach Jackie Sherrill said at the time. "Nobody can do what he can do and nobody has done what he has done at the position. He's the best defensive player that's been around in a long, long time. Pro scouts tell me he's the most productive football player in America per snap."

Despite all that, Green wouldn't win the Heisman, though he had a theory going in. With safeties Ronnie Lott (USC) and Kenny Easley (UCLA), both like Green having been mainstays in their programs and in the national spotlight, maybe there were enough great defensive options to change voters' mindsets.

"We had positioned ourselves defensively that if I didn't win the Heisman someone else defensively would have won it," Green said. "I was just one step in front of them, they had to sit and wait and they had to sit and gnaw the bone, because I was there with them in their class and doing the things that I had to do. . . . If you eliminate me then—BOOM!—it falls into the category of, 'OK, if I'm not deserving, then those guys are deserving.' One of the three."

But the trophy, as his defensive coordinator predicted, went to an offensive player: South Carolina senior running back George Rogers. The nation's leading rusher, Rogers won by 267 points over Green, who had to settle for second, with Georgia's freshman running back Herschel Walker in third (that's another contested part of this vote we'll get into later).

Green, at least, could perhaps take solace in a 37–9 rout of Rogers and the Gamecocks in the Gator Bowl that lifted the Panthers to No. 2 in the final AP Top 25. It was just the second time the top two vote-getters in balloting had ever met in a bowl—following Archie Griffin and Anthony Davis in 1974—and stands as one of six occasions over-all. While Rogers ran for 113 yards on 27 carries, he fumbled three times, losing two of them. Green was limited to 5 tackles, but South Carolina rarely ran at him and he was double-teamed for most of the night, leaving the Panthers' other defensive end, Ricky Jackson, free to make 19 stops.

"Hands-down in that category, I wanted the competition," Green said. "I wanted the spotlight. I wanted it to be between me and George, but again, I was mature enough to know because of offensive dictation and their respect of me, they were like 'Well, we're not going to run at the guy' and they didn't. You don't run at me or attack me, I had to take the glory of us defensively doing what we did to shut him down and beat them like we beat them with him being the Heisman."

The Heisman has forever been the playground of running backs and quarterbacks, with the former winning forty-two times, and the latter thirty-two. While two wide receivers—Tim Brown in 1987 and Des-mond Howard in '91—and a pair of tight ends—Larry Kelley (1936) and Leon Hart ('48)—are also a part of the fraternity, the votership has long had a narrow focus. As Ohio State's Chris Ward said when accept-ing the short-lived Downtown Athletic Club's Best Offensive Lineman Award at the 1977 Heisman ceremony, "I'd also like to accept this award on behalf of the offensive linemen in the United States, because I feel like there's only a few keen eyes that really watch what an offen-sive lineman does." Decades later, offensive linemen would still get no closer to the country's top award than did tackle John Hicks, another Buckeye, coming in second in 1973.

Defensive linemen, cornerbacks, and then some. The list of those positions that seem to lack a chance at receiving the award seems to go on and on. A winner that doesn't play one of those positions of power in running back or quarterback is nearly unthinkable, which has made one name stand out more than any other when it comes to truly breaking the stiff-armed mold: Charles Woodson.

The Michigan defensive back is credited as being the first defensive player to win the Heisman when he topped Tennessee's Peyton Manning by 272 points in 1997 and won five of the six regions, with Manning taking his home sector, the South. But Woodson didn't receive the trophy simply for his exploits at cornerback. Along with his 43 tackles, 7 interceptions, and 5 pass break-ups at the time of voting, the Wolverine had 11 receptions for 231 yards and 2 scores and returned 33 punts for 283 yards and a touchdown.

Woodson put it all on display November 22 against rival Ohio State, when he picked off a pass in the end zone, had a 37-yard reception to set up a score, and ran a punt back 78 yards for a touchdown. As he sat at the Downtown Athletic Club weeks later, Woodson said to himself, *Do I really have a shot?*

ESPN has taken heat over the years from Volunteers fans for the way it was believed to be waging an on-air campaign for the underdog Woodson, most notably on its College GameDay show, coming at the expense of Manning, who had thrown for 3,819 yards and 36 touchdowns in leading Tennessee to an SEC crown and over his career set 33 school records.

At the time, ESPN was showing Big Ten games and not SEC games, and after the ceremony, the network received angry telephone calls from Tennessee fans. Host Chris Fowler received a FedEx box filled with manure. Fowler responded by calling Vols fans "trailer-park trash"—he has since apologized—and further addressed the conspiracy charges years later in the oral history of ESPN, *Those Guys Have All the Fun.*

"People assumed Peyton Manning had the Heisman won. All I said was that this wasn't a done deal," he said. "I wasn't trying to hype Charles Woodson or the show for that matter. The show was going to rate what it rated. I was just doing my job."

Whether by design or not, Fowler and his employer weren't alone in the perceived pushing of Woodson, as Riska was quoted as saying, "Speaking for myself, I'd like to see a player like Woodson win it. I think it would be good, not only for the Heisman Trophy, but for college football."

He later refuted that endorsement, telling the *New York Times*, "I didn't say we wanted him to win. I said if he should turn out to be the winner, it would be good for college football. It would dispel the claim that there is a wall for defensive players.

"That's not saying that Peyton Manning or Ryan Leaf or Randy Moss wouldn't be good. I didn't mean it that way."

After receiving the Heisman, an emotional Woodson, who received 433 first-place votes to Manning's 281, said, "Defensive players can now go out and play their games. This has opened doors."

Not exactly.

Woodson was, in essence, a throwback to the days before the two-platoon system, when players saw significant time on both sides of the ball. To consider him strictly a defender in regards to his Heisman Trophy win would be to undermine his impact, overestimate the voters for focusing on the other side of the ball, and demean those who couldn't break through based solely on defense.

Green believes there was a sense of making up for bypassing him nearly two decades before.

"I just think that it was such a guilt factor in general that I didn't get it and people felt that, 'Oh, he should have got it. If anybody in the world [on defense] should have got it and he didn't get it,'" Green said. ". . . I should have got it before him in general. All I did was just make it more serious to give it to a defensive player . . . but he was returning punts and doing this and doing all that. So that sort of made it easy, so in their gesture or in their half-guiltiness they felt like, 'We should have gave it years ago [to a defender]. Now we finally ran into another guy of that breed, so let's give it to him . . . and by the way, he also returns punts. He does something offensively.'"

Prior to 1965, in the one-platoon era, those who played offense always played defense, too. Hence the award's first winner Jay Berwanger through Larry Kelley, Clinton Frank, and on and on, all saw time on both sides of the ball. Oklahoma's Kurt Burris was second in 1954, as was Iowa's Alex Karras in '57, and Penn's Chuck Bednarik finished third in '48, but Burris was a linebacker along with center, Bednarik played those same positions, and Karras balanced defensive tackle duties by also being a right guard.

UCLA's Moomaw won the Far West in '52, and while he's in the College Football Hall of Fame largely as a linebacker, like Bednarik and Burris, he was a center as well.

In the era of specialists (after the NCAA allowed teams to separate offense, defense, and special teams following the 1964 season), Nebraska's Rich Glover was the first pure defender to truly make noise in the Heisman voting. He was third in 1972, coming in 658 points behind teammate and winner Johnny Rodgers (adding to the firsts, Rodgers was the forefather to Johnny Manziel and Jameis Winston, bringing moral character into the equation with his involvement in a service station holdup as a freshman, along with driving with a suspended license).

While Oklahoma linebacker Brian Bosworth earned the first trip to New York in 1986 after the DAC began inviting the finalists, he came in fourth that year, as did Washington defensive tackle Steve Emtman ('91). Miami defensive tackle Warren Sapp ('94), Cornhuskers defensive tackle Ndamukong Suh ('09), and LSU's Tyrann Mathieu ('11) all made the ceremony as well, but no one could get higher than Suh's fourth, which included claiming the Southwest.

"I started as a freshman and played every game for four years and established my credentials so I had a chance," Green told Rivals.com in 2006. "Today for a defensive player to start as a freshman and go throughout his career, not leave early for the pros, etc. I don't think a pure defensive player can win."

Of that aforementioned group of finalists, only Suh was a senior (Bosworth, Emtman, Sapp, and Mathieu all would leave early for the

NFL), but he was largely a backup in his redshirt freshman season. Doing what Green couldn't would likely take a perfect storm, one that nearly came courtesy of Manti Te'o.

The linebacker had name recognition as a freshman All-American in '09 and a second-team All-American as a sophomore and junior. He was also at one of college football's most storied programs in Notre Dame, the launching pad for seven Heisman-winning careers, and was the poster boy for its revival under coach Brian Kelly, as the Fighting Irish earned a spot in the penultimate BCS National Championship Game.

He also had a captivating and heartbreaking narrative, with Te'o recounting to many media outlets how his seventy-two-year-old grandmother, Annette Santiago, and girlfriend Lennay Kekua—a student at Stanford—had both died on September 11, 2012. After receiving the news, he went out and racked up 12 tackles in a 20–3 upset of Michigan State.

With that backstory, 103 tackles and 7 interceptions (second most in FBS), when Heisman ballots were due, Te'o became part of a difficult choice for voters. Would they, for the first time, side with a freshman—to be clear, a redshirt—in Texas A&M's Johnny Manziel; a player who never saw an offensive snap in Te'o; or Kansas State's Collin Klein, the safe pick as a redshirt senior but whose campaign fell on its face in the final month?

Te'o claimed the Midwest and finished second in every other region behind 321 first-place votes, but came in 323 points behind Manziel, while Klein, the third finalist, registered just 60 firsts and was 1,135 behind the winner. Te'o didn't leave with the trophy, but he did, however, earn 1,706 points, a record for a defender.

Though there was no solace in that for the player whom he tied for the highest finish for a defender, Hugh Green.

"I didn't think that Manti Te'o was a player that really deserved the Heisman," Green said. "I thought that they tried to give it to him because of where he went, which was Notre Dame, the status of them as a school. If he won the Heisman, I'd still have the same opinion that they still didn't give the best defensive player the trophy, whereas offensively, they do. . . . Manti Te'o had [5] sacks. That's not an outstanding year. The defense did some things as a team, but individually, no."

We now know Te'o winning would have put the Heisman through an embarrassing scandal, more so than the off-the-field exploits of Johnny Football. Kekua never existed and the Notre Dame star had been "catfished," a term stemming from the 2010 Nev Schulman documentary *Catfish*, about a New Yorker who tracked down a woman he met online. She turned out to be a completely different person than whom he thought he'd been involved with.

Te'o had been duped by a man, Ronaiah Tuiasosopo, who had been disguising his voice in phone calls and made the linebacker believe he was Kekua. The two had never actually met and it was later discovered that Lennay Kekua never actually existed.

On the day of the ceremony, which came two days after Te'o found out his girlfriend had been a hoax, he perpetuated the storyline, telling a group of reporters, "I don't like cancer at all. I lost both my grandparents and my girlfriend to cancer."

As he told *Vanity Fair* months later: "Put yourself in my position. I've just found out my girlfriend is a big prank. And I think she's just died and people are asking me about her. And I'm just a twenty-one-year-old guy getting this question on a national stage just two days after it happens."

Victim or not, in breaking through the glass ceiling, youth, represented by Manziel, ended up saving the Heisman from being at the center of a public relations nightmare. A funny thought given the way age has long been viewed among voters.

Bias No. 3: Age

George Rogers was a fine and rather safe pick in 1980. But like its place in the offense vs. defense debate, no Heisman race is more closely dissected than when the topic of ageism is broached.

Rogers had more rushing yards than anyone at the time of voting—1,781 off a 6.0 average per carry—and held a streak of 21 consecutive games of 100 or more yards in a period when running backs were in the midst of hoisting the Heisman in 11 consecutive years.

The South Carolina star was also a senior, and had name recognition, rushing for 1,548 yards as a junior and finishing seventh in the balloting. Rogers's backstory didn't hurt either, as his father—George Sr.—left home when Jr. was around six, and in 1972 was convicted of murdering a woman he was living with. As he later recounted to UPI, the two had gotten into an argument and she was shot when a gun he had in his pocket fired. Meanwhile, George Jr. and his four siblings moved around the Atlanta area, living in eight towns in all before he moved in with his great aunt.

George Sr. had been sentenced to life, but was paroled after eight years, and released just ten days before his son and the No. 14 Gamecocks took on freshman Herschel Walker and fourth-ranked Georgia on November 1. It would be the first time George Sr. had ever seen his son play.

It also marked Rogers's first game on national television, and while the meeting of father and son in the locker room drew media attention, the day belonged to Walker and the Bulldogs.

Walker piled up 219 yards, 76 of which came on a touchdown run on the third play of the third quarter, lifting Georgia to a 13–10 win. Rogers didn't exactly struggle–running for 168 yards–but in the spotlight for the first time, and with the storybook platform of his father watching from the stands, the South Carolina star ceded the spotlight to Walker.

What began with Larry Munson's famous "My God, a freshman" call on the Georgia running back's first career touchdown run in a come-from-behind 16–15 win at Tennessee, and continued with a school-record 283 yards vs. Vanderbilt in a 41–0 rout October 18 was amplified in Walker's first test against a ranked opponent.

South Carolina provided him with a stage against a top-25 opponent and it provided him with a stage to run his season total to 1,096 yards and 10 scores through eight games, all that despite missing most of two with a sprained ankle.

"I don't think it was a battle between George and myself," Walker said after the win. "It was a battle between two great teams. It does not matter that I outgained George Rogers. What matters is that we won."

In terms of the Heisman, though, it should have ultimately been all that mattered, but Walker had to settle for third behind Rogers and Green. The Gamecock won Walker's own region (the South), while the freshman was third in the Northeast, Mid-Atlantic, and Far West and fifth in the Midwest.

"Even though Herschel outdueled him in that ballgame that we had, old George had been around for about four years," said Georgia coach Vince Dooley. "So I think the voters' mode of operation was to be based on not just a year, a freshman or a sophomore year, but somebody who had done it over the long haul. In light of that I was not surprised that Herschel didn't win it, but this day and time he would probably win it."

Walker would have to wait two more years to finally get his trophy, coming in second the following year behind 2,000-yard rusher Marcus Allen of USC. It's that 1980 vote that sticks out, given the way he captivated a nation.

Walker's 43 carries against the Gamecocks were a single-game Georgia record and he continued one of the finest freshman seasons in history, as he finished with 1,616 yards and 15 touchdowns, shattering the previous mark of 1,556 yards for a first-year player set by Pitt's Tony Dorsett in 1973.

While Rogers had 278 more yards, Walker boasted four 200-yard games to Rogers's one—two of which came on national TV—while getting just 9 carries against TCU and 11 vs. Ole Miss with the ankle injury. The phenom also powered the Bulldogs to an 11–0 record and an eventual national championship, while Rogers and South Carolina lost three games in all, including a 27–6 drubbing at the hands of Clemson (a defeat in which Rogers still had 168 yards).

The message was clear: underclassmen don't win Heismans.

"It's just such a stretch to believe that a freshman is going to win it, I don't think that anybody expected that it was going to happen, but it didn't change the feeling that he was the best player in the country," said Georgia quarterback Buck Belue. "That's sort of the way that the team looked at it."

A senior won every year for the first decade of balloting, with Army's Doc Blanchard standing as the first junior recipient in 1945, and seven seasons passed before a sophomore—Notre Dame's Angelo Bertelli (second in '41)—joined the top vote-getters. It was only due to freshmen being eligible because of World War II that Georgia Tech's Frank Castleberry came in third in 1942. After 1972, the first season that freshmen were again allowed to play varsity, Walker would be the first to mount a serious challenge.

Even Dorsett in the previous record-setting season for a freshman running back made the top five in just one region—fourth in his home sector, the East—making what Walker did all the more stunning, even if he didn't win.

"I guess I was realistic enough to understand the situation," Dooley says in hindsight. "I was, of course, disappointed for Herschel, hoping he'd win it as a freshman, but I had a broad perspective of what was going on."

George Rogers, by no fault of his own, became testament to the pedestal prolific juniors and seniors were placed upon, as did Oklahoma's Jason White when the quarterback beat out Pitt sophomore wide receiver Larry Fitzgerald in 2003. Walker only tied for the best finish by a first-year player in 1980 with Castleberry (1942), a mark that would be equaled by Virginia Tech's Michael Vick in 1999, and surpassed by Oklahoma's Adrian Peterson in 2004 when he came in second behind USC's Matt Leinart.

But if the last decade has been defined by any trend in voting, it's that age has become nearly a non-issue.

The rise in the number of players leaving early for the NFL has played a part. In the first ten years after the NFL began allowing anyone who is at least three years removed from high school to declare for the draft, an average of forty-nine players left school, but in the last eleven that's jumped to sixty-four, including a record 102 in 2014.

That's put the onus on younger players to contribute right away, many of whom have graduated from high school and enrolled early, though it doesn't completely account for the way Tim Tebow broke onto the national scene in 2006. While playing a part-time, but memorable, role in Florida's 2006 championship season, the situational

Florida's Tim Tebow broke through for underclassmen when he became the first sophomore winner in 2007.
(By Jameskpoole, via Wikimedia Commons)

runner became a household name and the following year became the first sophomore winner.

He would win five of the six regions, with the Southwest going to runner-up Darren McFadden (Arkansas), in a balloting dominated by upperclassmen, who racked up nine of the top ten spots. The first major college quarterback with 20 passing and 20 rushing touchdowns scored in a season, that 254-point margin of victory may have been even greater were he an upperclassman.

"There are a lot of great freshmen and sophomores out there," Tebow said that night. "And I'm just glad that I get to be the first one to win this."

The Gators quarterback started a trend, as suddenly it wasn't just OK to crown a sophomore—with Oklahoma's Sam Bradford and Alabama's Mark Ingram winning the next two seasons—it was acceptable to get behind them in droves.

In 2010, redshirt junior Cam Newton won for Auburn, a victory that broke the run by second-year players. But he was followed in the voting by two redshirt sophomores in Andrew Luck (Stanford) and LaMichael James (Oregon), with another in fifth (Oklahoma State's Justin Blackmon) and a true sophomore, Michigan's Denard Robinson, in sixth.

Then in '12, something happened that seemed implausible when Walker was denied in that historic 1980 campaign: Redshirt Manziel delivered for the freshman class. Then Florida State's Jameis Winston (another redshirt) delivered another for first-years the next season.

"That barrier's broken now," Manziel said upon winning. "It's starting to become more of a trend that freshmen are coming in early and that they are ready to play. And they are really just taking the world by storm."

The run was stopped there, as Alabama junior running back Derrick Henry claimed the 2015 prize. But even that vote showed the overall power youth is holding in this current climate.

Stanford's Christian McCaffrey came in second, with Clemson's Deshaun Watson third, LSU's Leonard Fournette sixth, and Florida

State's Dalvin Cook seventh, all of them sophomores. While that group helped '15 tie the '06 and '10 votes for the fewest number of upper-classmen in the top 10 with six, never before had four players who were less than two years removed from high school graduation finished in the top seven.

Bias No. 4: School

At a time when nearly every college football game is available on television—either nationally or regionally—or able to be streamed on a litany of devices, the very idea of a Heisman Trophy winner that the vast majority of voters have never seen so much as a highlight of seems far-fetched.

But in 1988, the NCAA, after investigating more than 250 charges of violations in recruiting, placed Houston on three years' probation and barred it from playing in bowl games for two. It also barred the Cougars from playing on TV for the 1989 season, creating the surreal, and somewhat ironic, scene of Andre Ware's first appearance coming via satellite, as the Heisman winner that season.

"We've overcome a lot as a football team, so I'm accepting this for my teammates at the University of Houston," Ware said during a cameo on CBS's live telecast of the Heisman announcement. He had just led the Cougars to a 64–0 rout of Rice in which he threw for 400 yards and two scores, hence his absence from the proceedings.

"This just shows that anything is possible at the beginning of the season; who would believe I would be sitting here today accepting the Heisman Trophy?"

Ware was unseen, but the numbers largely proved too mind-boggling to ignore, even if Ware played in the kind of program that had never won before and had never been closer than when Cornell's Ed Marinaro finished second in 1971.

Ware set twenty-six single-season NCAA records, including passing yards (4,699) and total offense (4,661) and completions (365), while throwing 46 touchdowns in leading a Cougars' run-and-shoot offense that averaged 53.5 points per game. So dominant was Houston in rolling through the Southwest Conference that Ware sat out eight quarters with the Cougars holding massive leads.

"There's always been the dark cloud of university probation, but I think the voters are aware now that I had absolutely nothing to do with it," Ware told the *Washington Post* the day before the ceremony. "Hopefully, if they vote for someone else, it's just because they think they are better than me."

But Ware had his doubters and critics because of stats that were the by-product of the pass-happy Air Raid offense (and likely, because Houston was facing that TV and postseason ban), a stance that was punctuated by his pass usage in a 40–24 win over Texas Tech. That was his final outing before votes were due, and the Cougars, junior passed on 63 of the team's 69 plays.

Nonetheless, he became the first winner on a team on probation, taking the South, Northeast, and Southwest, while Indiana running back Anthony Thompson claimed the Midwest and Far West and West Virginia's Major Harris won the Mid-Atlantic. Thompson finished 70 points back, making it, at the time, the fourth-closest vote ever.

"We weren't able to go to bowls this year," Cougars coach Jack Pardee told reporters. "This was our bowl game, Andre winning for himself and for the team."

Doc Blanchard's win as a junior in 1946 paved the way for three more players from that class in the next five years; likewise two more sophomores immediately followed Tim Tebow, and Johnny Manziel gave way to another redshirt freshman the season after his victory.

Ware's victory also opened the door, with Ty Detmer taking all six regions in 1990 in a season that one-upped Ware's. The BYU junior passed for 5,188 yards and 41 scores and boasted a résumé that included a win over top-ranked Miami that September.

"You try to picture yourself in this position, but you really can't imagine it," Detmer told CBS. Like Ware, he appeared on the Heisman telecast via satellite with the Cougars playing in Honolulu.

Said Cougars coach LaVell Edwards, who couldn't break through with previous quarterbacks Gifford Nielsen (sixth in 1976), Marc Wilson (third in '79), Jim McMahon (fifth in '80 and third in '81), Steve Young (second in '83), and Robbie Bosco (third in '84 and '85), "I think at that time it was a combination of not anybody else was really in his category and the fact that we had so many of them that were good quarterbacks, I think that helped him win the Heisman."

But Detmer's performances to follow that season, and the way Ware's successor was treated in voting, helped to set the stage for a new scrutiny for players from outside the power structure.

Hours after winning the Heisman, Detmer threw four interceptions and had a season-low 48.8 completion percentage (22 of 45) in a 59–28 loss to Hawaii, and followed that by being held to just 120 yards on 11 of 23 passing and one touchdown in a 65–14 rout at the hands of Texas A&M in the Holiday Bowl. He also ceded the single-season total offense record to Houston's new starter, David Klingler, who racked up 5,221 yards and 55 touchdowns.

Klingler was a Heisman finalist, but in a testament to how the numbers produced by the run-and-shoot were viewed, finished a distant fifth and managed just seven first-place votes to Detmer's 316.

A year later, Detmer was third to Michigan's Desmond Howard after a dismal start in three straight losses to Top 25 teams, drawing 445 points to the wide receiver's 2,077, and was even third in his own voting region—the Far West—coming in behind Howard and Washington's Steve Emtman.

Those who played on a perceived lesser stage—which included the service academies, winners of five Heismans between 1945–63—simply couldn't break through any longer. It was a point driven home by Marinaro's narrow loss to Auburn's Pat Sullivan in '71, despite the Cornell back leading the nation in rushing in back-to-back seasons; and it was there when San Diego State's Marshall Faulk, the country's top rusher in 1991 and '92, was a distant second to Miami's Gino Torretta in '92.

Faulk's being a sophomore may have played a part, as did the love affair with those Hurricanes teams for which Torretta was the latest poster boy, but the Aztecs' running back was 320 points behind Torretta, earning 164 first-place votes to the quarterback's 310.

In the years since, players from the ranks called mid-majors, and in the latest nomenclature, Group of Five, have become fixtures in the final vote tallies. Since 1994, two years—1995 and 2014—didn't include at least one of those players in the top 10 and in that stretch, eight of them have been finalists (Alcorn State's Steve McNair in '94, Marshall's Randy Moss in '97, the Thundering Herd's Chad Pennington in '95, TCU's LaDanian Tomlinson in 2000, Utah's Alex Smith in '04, Hawaii's Colt Brennan in '06, Boise State's Kellen Moore in '10, and Northern Illinois's Jordan Lynch in '13), but none have been closer than McNair's third place.

Being a quarterback or a running back can pave the way, as can being a junior or a senior or playing in a region with start times that can get a player eyeballs. But the team, and one's spot in the college football universe's pecking order, has become a major force in voting for the past twenty-five years, one that has only been magnified as everything else in the game orbited around the BCS, and now the College Football Playoff. A trip to New York seems to be the new ceiling for those who don't play in the ACC, Big Ten, Big 12, Pac-12, SEC, or don't suit up for Notre Dame.

Biases, in all their forms, make the process of defining *outstanding*, as votes both past and present assure us, full of limitations.

CHAPTER FOUR

HOW GRIFFIN STILL STANDS ALONE

THE REQUESTS POURED in, and Archie Griffin abided—again and again and again. He did interviews, attended banquets, visited hospitals, and spoke at schools. The Ohio State running back was, after all, an instant celebrity in Columbus, after winning the Heisman Trophy in 1974 as a junior. He didn't want to come off as cocky, and, to a fault, he simply couldn't say no.

"I got a ton of requests to do this, do that, and I was trying to do a lot of that stuff," Griffin said.

In stepped Woody Hayes.

The Buckeyes' legendary coach, forever tough and temperamental, called Griffin into his office. He was well aware of the many ways his star was being pulled.

"Hey, you cannot do everything for everybody," Hayes told him. "You can't please everybody. You've got to pay attention to your school and pay attention to what we're going to do out on the football field. It's going to make you soft."

Or, as Hayes even more colorfully said to the Associated Press before the September 13 opener against Michigan State in 1975, "He can't go to the bathroom without somebody wanting him to make a speech or interview him. We have to shield him. If we don't, it will take the edge off him. The coach will have to get mean. Arch can't be mean."

It was pure Hayes: insulating in his meaning, and blunt in his delivery, but it was the kind of guidance Griffin needed as he began a chase that would see him do what Doc Blanchard in 1946, Doak Walker ('49), Vic Janowicz ('51), Roger Staubach ('64), and every other Heisman winner to date had all failed to do: win a second trophy.

For forty years and counting, Griffin has stood alone, his phone ringing just a little bit more than often as nine players—most recently Florida State's Jameis Winston in 2014—have tried to match him, but to no avail. He remains steadfast that it will happen, and when it does, "I hope I can be the first to congratulate them," he said.

Breaking mindsets is difficult work in this underlying bias of voting, but just as Hayes was safeguarding player and program by telling his running back that it was OK to be mean, Griffin was telling voters that it's OK to give him an equal in a place in history that seems more and more unobtainable as time passes. "I will always have that designation of being first, and I'll be proud of that as well," Griffin said.

Long before he began his waiting game, Griffin simply needed reassurance that Mr. Nice Guy could break character.

"I appreciated those words, because I wasn't sure if I should be doing all those things for people, because I wanted to be helpful and it was hard to say 'No' at times," Griffin said. "But it helped me to know that my coach, if I said 'No' to people asking me to do something, that it was OK. Coach Hayes was a man that always talked about being able to help other people, but then he told me, 'You can't do everything for everybody,' so it helped me in handling those situations."

He learned to say 'No,' but try as his coach did to help Griffin keep his focus inward and not outward, Griffin couldn't help but still feel the pressure. Until he won in 1974, Griffin wasn't aware that none of the previous juniors to win had not been able to repeat, but, "Everyone's scaring it into me now," he said after being announced as the fortieth winner.

It was a point he'd become all too familiar with over the next twelve months, and as difficult as it seemed at the time—Blanchard was fourth in his follow up, Walker third, and Staubach, like Janowicz, didn't crack the Top 10—Griffin considered another lesson from Hayes.

"Coach Hayes used to have this saying, 'You're either getting better or you're getting worse. You never stay the same,'" Griffin said. "It was probably a little warped thinking on my part, but for me, to at least stay the same, I need to win the Heisman Trophy again."

He recalls an evening before the start of that senior season. While he was thumbing through the Bible, a feeling of the intensity of that repeat bid was weighing on him. "It was too much to put on a person, and I just turned it over to the Lord," Griffin said.

He came across Psalm 37:4, and found peace.

Delight yourself in the Lord and he will give you the desires of your heart.

"I remember when I read that verse, it was as if someone had taken a big weight off my shoulders," Griffin said. "That verse told me that my job was to find joy in serving the Lord, and if I did that, one of two things would happen. He'd take that desire away from me of winning the Heisman Trophy or he'd give it to me as a gift."

Griffin was, on the field, a marked man, as everyone wanted a crack at the reigning golden boy. On option plays, whether receiving the pitch or not, "you're going to get popped," he said. It was nothing dirty, but he recounts opponents taking shots at him after dropping him to the ground, saying things like "Get up, Heisman Trophy winner."

"Those type of things did happen, and I expected them to happen," Griffin said. "But it got harder."

And not just in the physical sense, as Griffin withstood that extra punishment. The caliber of challengers around him in what would become the Year of the Running Back added to the degree of difficulty in what Griffin was trying to accomplish.

In 1974, when Griffin ran for 1,620 yards in winning by a 1,101-point landslide over USC's Anthony Johnson, the two were among nine running backs across the country that had topped 1,100 yards in the regular season. A year later, there were twenty, including the Trojans' Ricky Bell—a 6-foot-2, 215-pound converted fullback whose 1,875 yards were six from breaking the record Cornell's Ed Marinaro set in '71; Cal's all-purpose monster Chuck Muncie (1,871 total yards); and Pitt's Tony Dorsett (1,544).

"There were some great running backs, no question, and I love all [those] guys, because they were impressive to me," Griffin said. "But I didn't really think that much about it; it was really about that job at hand that we had to do at Ohio State."

Griffin also had an important streak to maintain, of 100-yard games that dated back to the first months of his sophomore season. The face of the preseason's fourth-ranked team tore through No. 11 Michigan State to start the year, with 111 yards and three touchdowns on 29 carries, followed with 128 yards on 24 tries vs. No. 7 Penn State, and after a 157-yard day against North Carolina, steamrolled 13th-ranked UCLA for 160 yards and a score.

"There were people who thought that we could possibly lose those first four games because of the talent that we lost the year before and we had coming back," Griffin said.

His consistency helped propel the Buckeyes to No. 1 by October—a spot they'd maintain through an 11–0 regular season—and again positioned him as the trophy favorite.

It didn't hurt that there was no true consensus on who was the best option to dethrone him.

A November 1 meeting in Berkeley, California, was a chance to offer some clarity in the West, with Cal's Golden Bears knocking off the fourth-ranked USC Trojans 28–14. Muncie ran for 143 yards and had 62 more receiving, while Bell was limited to 122 yards, 34 below his season average.

Muncie ended up outrushing Griffin (1,460 yards to Griffin's 1,357), but Cal was a three-loss team, falling to No. 20 West Virginia and 19th-ranked UCLA, with the win over USC their only defeat of a ranked opponent. That didn't help his case, and neither did his not being the true focal point of the nation's top-ranked offense, which was averaging 458.5 yards per game. Quarterback Joe Roth, who didn't take over the job until the third game of the season, ended up fifth in the country with 1,880 passing yards.

Bell, despite losing head-to-head to Muncie on a Trojans team whose season was spiraling out of control, wasn't going to concede the region, either.

John McKay's announcement before the Cal game that he would be taking over the NFL's Tampa Bay Buccaneers rocked a program that would lose four straight. Bell still ran for 195 yards in a 13–10 loss to Stanford, and, with 190 in an 8–7 defeat to Washington the following game, had broken O. J. Simpson's single-season Pac 8 record of 1,739 yards. He entered the final week against the rival Bruins 143 from the all-time mark and settled on 136 and two touchdowns.

The West's contenders boiled down to two guys—the country's top rusher on a four-loss team in Bell, and Muncie, whose three-loss squad didn't get invited to a bowl game; the East had Dorsett, with a résumé that boasted a 303-yard day (the most ever allowed by Notre Dame), from a Pitt team with four defeats.

Then there was Griffin, the centerpiece of the top-ranked and unbeaten Buckeyes, the household name and model of consistency—though that last part did come to an end in the days before votes were due.

In the regular-season finale at eighth-ranked Michigan, Griffin was held to 46 yards on 19 carries, bringing an end to his streak of 100-yard games at 31. As he walked off the field after the 21–14 win, Griffin couldn't help but wonder if he'd cost himself the trophy.

"I did, no question," he said. "But at the same time, the big thing was we won the football game and that was most important. . . . I felt that people would appreciate the fact that you could go almost three full seasons with gaining 100 yards every game, which I think people appreciated and respected that kind of consistency and that would mean a lot."

He ran for 263 fewer yards than the year before, and five others ran for more yards, but Griffin would carry four of the five regions—with Muncie taking the Far West—in claiming 454 first-place votes and 1,800 points in all. In a show of how much dissension there was between Muncie and Bell, they were separated by just 22 points, with the Cal Bear second (730 points) and the Trojan third (708). Dorsett finished fourth with 616 points. Underscoring the Year of the Running Back, the position made up the top six, and seven of the first eight.

"Two Heismans—that puts him in a class all by himself," Hayes said succinctly at the ceremony.

Decades later, Hayes's words still ring true. Griffin remains alone in that class, each bid after his going awry, be it from injury, raised expectations, the rise of teammates, or—in this new age—scandal. The photo of Griffin posing with the trophy in 1975, wearing an ensemble that screams '70s—dark turtleneck with blazer and a gold chain hanging around his neck—and holding up two fingers, has taken on iconic status.

If a Heisman jinx truly exists, it resides in every attempt to try to claim that elusive second trophy.

"Obviously it's a hard thing to do, because I thought it would have happened by now and more than once by now," Griffin said.

1979: Billy Sims

"I'm not going to let down, Charles White, if you're listening," Oklahoma's Billy Sims said in the summer of 1979.

Of course, White was listening.

The USC running back, along with Sims, Tennessee's Roland James, Texas's Steve McMichael, and North Carolina State's Jim Ritcher, was on a week-long college football promotional tour co-sponsored by the National Collegiate Athletic Association and ABC. What began at the College Football Hall of Fame, then near Kings Island amusement park in Ohio, took them from New York to New Orleans, Dallas, and Los Angeles before finishing in San Francisco.

Sims and White were the biggest attractions. The Sooners running back stood as the reigning Heisman winner, while the Trojan was the nation's leading rusher in 1978 and finished fourth in the voting.

Be it the fact that he was traveling alongside the trophy winner, or that he ran for 97 more yards than Sims and had to watch him hoist the trophy, White's focus was clear.

"Yes, I think about the Heisman," he told reporters.

Aside from his message to White—and a *Sports Illustrated* cover in which the two were in a tug of war with the trophy under the headline "Hey, Man, That's My Heisman!"—Sims wasn't letting on that the Heisman was in his thoughts. He had, quite literally, come out of nowhere to win the award as a junior. After just 71 carries for 413 yards as a sophomore, Sims broke out in the Sooners' wishbone offense for 1,762 yards and 20 touchdowns and topped the vote by a mere 77 points over Penn State quarterback Chuck Fusina. The vote was so close that the New York accounting firm of Harris, Kerr, Forster and Co. had to count the ballots for a second time.

Now the possibility of equaling Griffin hung there, but Sims had a take-it-or-leave-it attitude about the chase.

"A lot of people ask me, 'What are your chances of winning the Heisman again?'" Sims said. "I just tell them that last season I was sort of an unknown running back and I really wasn't in the game to win the Heisman Trophy and I'm not going for it again this year. But if it happens, fine."

Just four years removed from Griffin winning his second, the feat had nowhere near the same mystique it does today, and at that point it was overshadowed by the former Buckeye's struggles in the NFL. Taken with the 24th pick in the 1976 draft by the Cincinnati Bengals, Griffin never came close to that benchmark figure of 1,000 yards in a season, with his best season coming in 1979 when he ran for 688 on 140 carries.

So from Sims's standpoint, being on the same footing as Griffin wasn't a precursor for success.

"I don't know what it would mean," Sims told the Associated Press in 1979 of a second win. "Besides, look at Archie Griffin. So what is he doing now with two Heisman trophies?"

For the second straight year he was a consensus All-American, was once again the Big Eight Player of the Year, and in the final two games of the season he ran for 529 yards, including a career-high 282 against Missouri (and a week later he had 247 in a 17–14 victory over third-ranked Nebraska). But Sims would become a victim of the microscope under which reigning winners are placed, where any blemish on a résumé becomes a major focus.

What one might call the Sooners running back's "blemish" came October 13 when No. 4 Texas held him to just 73 yards on 20 carries in a 16–7 loss. It snapped a 14-game streak of 100-yard games and in that defeat, Sims didn't have a single run over 16 yards. Asked afterward if he believed it cost him the Heisman, Sims replied, "I don't care. I have one already."

He may have been able to overcome it if he had lifted Oklahoma into national title contention as a senior, but heading into the voting the team was fifth at 10-1-0. Meanwhile, White had nearly 300 more yards at 1,803, fueled by a national record of 1,090 in five straight games, and his Trojans were sitting second in the AP Top 25, a Rose Bowl date with Ohio State looming.

White won comfortably, picking up 453 first-place votes to Sims's 82, with 992 points separating the two. Sims was unavailable for comment at the time of the announcement, but coach Barry Switzer opened up, showing frustration with the voting process. He believed that professional scouts, not media members, should award the Heisman, though he also laid out the grim reality facing anyone making a chase at Griffin's record: the heightened expectations.

"He's had a better year than any other Heisman winner trying to repeat," Switzer said. "His two years were better than Archie Griffin's two years he won the thing."

Years later, Griffin admits that he thought that Sims was going to join him. "I certainly thought he would," he said, "and he had a great chance." Arguably, Sims had a better chance than anyone in history, even if unlike modern-day winners he only had one opportunity to go for No. 2. But the worst thing that would happen to repeat bids is time, and more than a decade would pass before anyone made another run at Griffin.

1991: Ty Detmer

It came as little surprise that Herschel Walker left Georgia for the USFL after his Heisman-winning junior season in of 1982, especially with some wondering if after his freshman year he would challenge the NFL's rule (at the time) of not admitting players until their class had graduated. Given the fact that the next two juniors to claim the award, Barry Sanders in 1988 and Andre Ware a year later, flipped on their initial comments about sticking around and bolted for the pros, there was obvious skepticism when BYU's Ty Detmer said days after claiming the '90 trophy that "I made a commitment to the school and I believe in living up to that."

He didn't balk, and the game had its first returning winner since Sims twelve years earlier in a quarterback who had broken twenty-one national total offense records, twenty-one passing records, and tied five more in throwing for 5,188 yards and 41 touchdowns. With 1990 runner-up Notre Dame's Raghib Ismail bolting after his junior year, Houston's David Klingler (fifth) was the only player joining Detmer in the top 10 in voting who was back on campus in 1991.

Detmer was set up to be the heavy favorite as a senior, though in reality, that bid may have ended before it ever even started.

His stock had already taken a hit during his junior campaign with debacles against Hawaii—that one coming the day he was given the award—and Texas A&M in the Holiday Bowl, and when coach LaVell Edwards met with Detmer before the season, he delivered a message of putting the past in the past, one that could be seen as twofold given those highs and lows.

"The worst thing you can do is feel like you have to live up to the year before," Edwards told his quarterback. "Try to get that out of your mind and do the best you can now. Win as many games as you can and be as effective as you can."

Unfortunately for his hopes of winning a second trophy, he was anything but effective.

In the 19th-ranked Cougars' season-opening 44–28 loss to No. 1 Florida State in the Pigskin Classic, Detmer was held without a touchdown pass through three and a half quarters before throwing two in the final eight minutes. He threw for 229 yards and an interception, which was his 15th in the last six games dating back to '90 as BYU slipped to 25th.

A week later against No. 23 UCLA, Detmer did throw for 377 yards, 2 scores, and 2 more interceptions, and broke the career passing yardage of San Diego State's Todd Santos with a five-yard pass to Micah Matsuzaki in the second quarter. It wasn't enough, though, with a 27–23 defeat knocking BYU out of the Top 25.

The setbacks continued the next time out vs. No. 12 Penn State, which sacked Detmer 6 times and limited him to 158 yards on just 8 completions.

If there was a silver lining, it was that after that skid—which gave the Cougars their longest losing streak since they lost four straight between the 1974 and '75 seasons—few were paying attention anymore.

"I wasn't under a microscope this year," Detmer told the AP that November. "That really made it nice."

Statistically, he rebounded, finishing with 4,031 yards and 35 touchdowns to 12 picks, punctuated by leading the Cougars to a 52–52 tie with San Diego State after trailing by 28. Detmer connected on 4 of his 6 touchdown passes in the final twenty minutes in throwing for a school-record 599 yards.

Detmer was heading back to New York as a finalist, but it wasn't even close. As the quarterback said days before the ceremony, "I'm going to New York to watch Desmond."

That would be Michigan's Desmond Howard, who gobbled up 640 first-place votes, while the reigning winner had just 19 in coming in third, 1,632 points behind the wide receiver, with Florida State's Casey Weldon in second.

That amounted to the largest margin of victory in any contest since O. J. Simpson won by 1,750 points in '68 and still stands as the biggest in any vote in which another Heisman winner was in the field.

"The expectations were just too high," Detmer said of his failed bid. "Every game had to be better than the previous one."

2004: Jason White

Never mind Archie Griffin. Jason White was thinking about Army's Doc Blanchard and Glenn Davis.

They were the only teammates to claim the Heisman in back-to-back years—1945 and '46. In 2004, the Oklahoma quarterback—on campus for a sixth season after he was granted another year of eligibility for a medical hardship as he underwent knee surgeries in 2001 and '02—had designs on joining them.

Asked that October in a press conference whether he or the Sooners' breakout freshman running back Adrian Peterson should be getting more attention, White didn't hesitate.

"Adrian," he said.

The way White saw it, he already had his trophy, edging out Pitt wide receiver Larry Fitzgerald by a mere 76 points in 2003 behind the strength of 396 first-place votes. He had returned to Norman to win a Big 12 championship and a national title, not for a second Heisman. But being able to hand off—figuratively and literally—to another trophy recipient was far too unique of an opportunity, so he opted to deflect the Heisman hype.

"He came in and just kind of took over. He was a freshman that year and was playing really well," White said of Peterson. "I thought it would be super special to be a teammate of a guy that had won one also."

Two players on the same team in the top 10 in voting was far from unprecedented, though there was the possibility of blocking each other in this popularity contest.

After 1946, twenty-nine times teammates finished in the top 10 together, and on eight occasions—Michigan's Leon Hart (1949), Oklahoma's Billy Vessels (1952), Notre Dame's John Huarte (1964), Nebraska's Johnny Rodgers (1972), USC's Charles White (1979), the Cornhuskers' Mike Rozier (1983), Miami's Gino Torretta (1992), and Ohio State's Eddie George (1995)—one of them won the trophy.

White, though, was dealing with a situation that just one player, Blanchard, could understand. The Cadets' halfback was the only other returning winner who finished behind a player from his own team in voting—coming in fourth as a senior—and here was White, publicly pushing for the same fate.

"I just thought [it] would be very unique and you couldn't ask for a better guy to win it than Adrian, because he worked so hard [and] he was a freshman, just out of high school," White said.

It was more of the personal anti-promotion for a player who, when asked to replicate the 1979 White-Sims *SI* cover with USC's Matt Leinart—the preseason favorite—refused. Granted, White's numbers were down overall, throwing for 2,961 yards and 33 touchdowns, whereas he helped the Sooners to a 12–0 regular season and a spot opposite the Trojans in the Orange Bowl for the Bowl Championship Series title, after racking up 3,744 and 40, respectively, the year before. Nevertheless, over White's last six games of his Sooners career, he tossed 21 touchdown passes and just one interception.

That late surge certainly had something to do with Peterson, who ran for 1,843 yards and 15 scores. As defenses keyed in on stopping him, White took advantage, and it was he, not the freshman running back, who was named the Big 12 Offensive Player of the Year.

White was back in New York that December, along with Peterson, Leinart and his USC teammate Reggie Bush, and Utah's Alex Smith as finalists. It was a far more relaxed feel for the Sooners quarterback, because "I knew 'Hey, we're going to do this, this, and this, and after that, we get to do this,'" White said. "The year before I was constantly asking people 'OK, what are we going to do next? What am I supposed to wear?' It was just a lot more fun the next year."

He had the confidence of Griffin, who days before the ceremony said, "I'll be awfully proud of Jason," but not that of the nation's pollsters, as White finished third behind Leinart in first and Peterson in second.

White was resigned to his finish before the ballots were even counted, saying, "I pretty much knew the people that were up for the Heisman Trophy that year; it would have been tough to win it regardless, just because of the athletes that were in it and the great seasons they had."

It's hard to argue, though, that vote-splitting didn't play a role.

The concept, given the 3-2-1 ballot, is a subjective topic, as the format would seem to dissuade it. But we're talking about a vote where Leinart came in first (1,325), with Peterson second (997) and White third (957), and that 328-point margin of victory could have become much tighter or even flipped if just one Sooner was vying for attention.

Had Peterson absorbed White's points, or vice versa, either one would have won handily. Even if we just remove either player from the Southwest (given the Oklahoma players' dominance there, and that there was only one other player from that region in the top 10 in voting in Texas's Cedric Benson, who was sixth), it's conceivable they would have collected the brunt of the region's first-place votes. White had 171 in all, representing 513 of his points, and Peterson drew 154 for 462 points. Put either of those totals toward the other Sooner, and we're talking another Heisman for Oklahoma, and in the case of White, an equal for Griffin.

Instead, Leinart won, and set the stage for nearly an identical story to play itself out the following season in Troy.

2005: Matt Leinart

That Leinart was even returning to USC as a senior was stunning. He followed up that 2004 Heisman season by throwing for five touchdowns in a 55–19 rout of Oklahoma in the Orange Bowl and was expected to be one of the top, if not *the* top, pick in the NFL draft, but Leinart passed it all up to come back to USC for one more season.

As he addressed a crowd of roughly 500 inside the Trojans' Heritage Hall, he joked of the multi-million-dollar payday he was delaying. "I get $950 a month," he said of his stipend, drawing laughter. "Come on, $950 a month. We've got a training table. We've got food."

He added, "The money is not important to me. I realize the opportunities. My teammates and being here is more important to me right now."

History seemed his and the Trojans' for the taking. They were coming off back-to-back national championships and eyeing an unprecedented third in a row with nine starters back on offense and fourteen starters back overall.

Winners of twenty-two straight games and a 36–3 over the course of the previous three seasons, those USC teams were celebrities in the world's playground for them, and they shared their stage with the rich and famous.

Will Ferrell, Jake Gyllenhaal, and Kirsten Dunst were spotted on the sidelines during games, as were André 3000, Snoop Dogg, and Dr. Dre.

"When you're sitting on the bench and you see George Lucas or Nick Lachey and Jessica Simpson cruise past, you're like 'Is that who I thought it was?'" linebacker Oscar Lua told *USA TODAY*.

With no professional football team in Los Angeles at the time, the Trojans basically *were* the city's de facto franchise. But this was more than that. In 2004, USC would set a Pac-10 record in drawing an average of 85,229 fans per game at home and in '05 they shattered that, pulling in 90,812 a game, and went over the million mark over the course of the season for the first time.

"It's pretty clear that USC football is the place to be," coach Pete Carroll told the school's website.

The hype couldn't have been more amplified or the path seemingly more clear.

In Leinart, college football boasted the poster boy of the nation's most dominant program, who was expected to put up monster numbers and lead his team in a perceived sprint to the BCS Championship. That final point was key, because with Leinart's win in '04, four of the previous five Heisman winners had all been quarterbacks who took their team to the title game. In an era where the marquee player on the best team won, Leinart fit the bill in 2004 and, it was presumed, again in '05.

"There's a lot of preseason hype about Archie Griffin being the only two-time winner of the Heisman, but everybody on our team knows that's not what I'm about," Leinart told the AP before that season.

Granted, Oklahoma's Adrian Peterson was back after finishing second to Leinart, but he would wind up taking himself out of the running. He missed one game—the Big 12 opener against Kansas State—and was limited in three others with a sprained right ankle. He still ran for 1,108 yards and 14 touchdowns, but since Notre Dame's Angelo Bertelli in 1939, who was activated by the Marine Corps after six games, only two winners have missed a game (Charles White in 1979 and Charlie Ward in '93).

It was going to take the truly spectacular to derail Leinart.

The quarterback's numbers improved that fall—he threw for 3,453 yards and 27 touchdowns at the time of the voting, which was 463 more yards than he went to New York with as a junior—in putting the Trojans in line to play for that third straight title. But for those looking for the truly spectacular, running back Reggie Bush supplied it.

He ran for 1,685 yards on just 187 carries, a stunning 8.9 average, and led the nation with 2,611 all-purpose yards, which amounted to

217.5 per game. It was all on display in a 50–42 scare (an eventual USC victory) from No. 16 Fresno State, in which Bush set a Pac-10 record with 513 yards and delivered his Heisman moment as he took a handoff with 1:27 to play in the third quarter, USC clinging to a 34–28 lead.

He broke through the left side of the offensive line and toward the sideline as one defender caught up to him at the 25-yard line, with two more just downfield. But instead of stepping out of bounds or cutting back inside, Bush simply stopped. Completely. The defender backpedaled, losing ground as the Trojan then changed direction and raced back inside for the 50-yard touchdown.

"He was pure magic," Carroll said that night.

"Reggie's got my vote," said Leinart—who, as a former winner, received his own ballot.

Unlike '04 when Peterson and White hurt one another by competing for attention, this was complete and utter domination. Bush claimed 784 of the 892 first-place votes and 91.7 of the maximum possible points—the most ever—while Texas's Vince Young was second (1,608) and Leinart third (797).

In retrospect, given the NCAA scandal that forced USC to forfeit games and, ultimately, Bush to return the trophy (which we'll get into later), along with Young stealing the Trojans' thunder and title in the Rose Bowl (also, a topic for a subsequent chapter), the question of whether or not Bush deserved to win has been up for discussion. But to underscore how little debate there was at the time, Young's 613 were the most second-place votes in history and Leinart's 18 first-place nods were the fewest of any returning winner.

That put USC alongside Notre Dame with a record-tying seventh Heisman, one for which Bush was quick to thank his quarterback.

"Matt, what more can I say?" Bush said. "Your decision to come back has changed my life."

2008, 2009: Tim Tebow

By virtue of being the first sophomore to win the Heisman, Florida quarterback Tim Tebow was mathematically the biggest threat to win a second trophy. But that's not entirely why he seemed destined to be Archie Griffin's equal.

He was seemingly too good to be true, a player who went from a relief role during the Gators' 2006 national title run to having coach Urban Meyer call him "the best quarterback of our era" after just one season as a starter.

A barreling runner and sidearmed left-handed passer, he was the perfect fit for Meyer's spread option offense, throwing for 3,132 yards and 29 touchdowns and just 6 picks, while rushing for 838 yards and 22 scores ahead of the 2007 Heisman ceremony.

Tim Tebow the player was Paul Bunyan in orange and blue. His legend was in the Jump Pass I—coming against LSU as a freshman—and II—which sealed the '08 national championship vs. Oklahoma. It was in The Promise—a 102-word declaration after a stunning 31–30 loss

On the topic of Heisman moments, that play that becomes the backbone of a campaign, here's a ranking of the five best: 5. Barry Sanders runs for 293 yards and 4 touchdowns—including an 80-yarder—on Iowa State in 1988; 4. Charles Woodson's 78-yard punt return for a touchdown against Ohio State in 1997; 3. Johnny Manziel scrambles, loses the ball, catches it, and still throws a 10-yard touchdown pass vs. Alabama in 2012; 2. Desmond Howard strikes the pose after a 93-yard punt return for a score against Ohio State; 1. Bush's stop/start.

Missing from that list? Doug Flutie's Hail Mary against defending national champion Miami in 1984. The Hail Flutie game occurred November 23, and while Flutie was that year's winner, this moment came after the voting deadline.

to unranked Ole Miss that paved the way to that '08 crown, and which is immortalized with a plaque outside the Florida football offices.

Tim Tebow the man wore his Christianity on his sleeve, and his morals like a coat of arms. When blindsided at SEC Media Days ahead of his senior season and asked if he was still a virgin—the exact phrase being "Are you saving yourself for marriage?"—a beet-red Tebow responded, "Yes I am." He was a miracle baby, his mother Pam contracting amoebic dysentery on a missionary trip to the Philippines and falling into a coma. She had no clue she was pregnant and the drugs doctors administered caused the placenta to detach, robbing her child of oxygen, a condition known as placental abruption. It was expected the baby had suffered brain damage and she was urged to abort the fetus.

"They thought I should have an abortion to save my life from the beginning all the way through the seventh month," Pam told the *Gainesville Sun* in 2007.

She refused, leaning on faith. As Bob Tebow told *Sports Illustrated* in 2009, "I prayed, 'God, if you give me a son, if you give me Timmy, I'll raise him to be a preacher.'"

Tim Tebow became exactly that, delivering sermons as a missionary in the Philippines, and months after winning the Heisman, while working at a clinic that his father runs in Southeast Asia, he performed circumcisions for impoverished children despite no formal training.

"The first time, it was nerve-racking," he told the *Orlando Sentinel* in the spring of 2008. "Hands were shaking a little bit. I mean, I'm cutting somebody. You can't do those kinds of things in the United States. But those people really needed the surgeries. We needed to help them."

Tim Tebow was the Heisman's Golden Boy redefined in the era of Twitter and a nonstop news cycle, and because he possessed a game that didn't look to translate to the NFL—with that herky-jerky throwing motion—he was no threat to bolt early for the pros.

As a junior he led the Gators to the national title game with 2,515 yards and 28 touchdowns through the air and 564 yards and 12 scores on the ground, but despite having more first-place votes than anyone (309), he lost to Oklahoma sophomore Sam Bradford (his opponent in that BCS finale). That marked the first time since Oklahoma's Tommy McDonald in 1956 that a player drew the most first-place votes and finished that far back.

Asked if it was any consolation, Tebow replied, "Not really. You lose, you lose."

By the time his senior year drew to a close—a season in which he and Florida were No. 1 up until losing the SEC Championship Game 32–13 to Alabama, ending any national title aspirations—the Tebow love affair had, in many ways, become Tebow Fatigue.

Teammates and coaches would often sing his praises and arguably no player in Florida history was more popular. Indiana basketball coach Tom Crean, for example, noted that he had used video of Tebow to motivate his team, calling the quarterback "toughness personified." But some had grown tired of his clean-cut persona, hence that virginity question ahead of his senior season.

"There've been moments, there've been days, when you get tired, you get frustrated, you get exhausted," Tebow told *USA TODAY* in December 2009. "You want people to believe you're doing things for the right reason, but sometimes people just look at the negative. 'It's fake. Or it's this or that.' That's when my faith really encourages me that everything happens for a reason and God has a plan."

The numbers—2,413 yards passing, 859 rushing, and a combined 31 scores—weren't enough to claim that final Heisman vote, but Tebow did become the only player invited to the ceremony three times. That in itself is interesting, looking back at the vote count.

Tebow was a distant fifth in 2009, behind Alabama's Mark Ingram, generating just 43 first-place votes and 390 points overall. He was a whopping 425 behind the fourth-place finisher, Nebraska's Ndamukong Suh. In the twenty-eight years of inviting contenders to New York, never had the Heisman dug so deep to include a player in a field of four-plus finalists. The 1990 ceremony came close, as Virginia's

Shawn Moore was 340 points ahead of the last finalist, Houston's David Klingler, but typically the cutoff had been around 200 points or less. But Tim Tebow was a former winner, and let's face it, a ratings draw in all his polarizing glory.

If anyone was going to win a second trophy, it was going to be Tebow, or at least it legitimately could have been Tebow. Those first-place votes in his junior season show us that the majority of voters were ready to finally put another on that pedestal. But there's also this nugget: his name only appeared on 750 of the 902 ballots cast, meaning 153 voters left him off completely.

Remarked Tebow that night after he finished third in '08: "They either love the Gators or they hate us."

2009: Sam Bradford; 2010: Mark Ingram

During his rookie season with the Denver Broncos in 2010, Tebow told an AP reporter that despite the outside hoopla, he never truly focused on winning another Heisman. It wasn't that he was immune to it, but at a program where anything but a national title was a failure, the trophy became secondary.

"If you were maybe somewhere else where you didn't have that pressure and that expectation of winning a championship, maybe the Heisman would affect you more," Tebow said. "But I don't think it really had an effect because of our level of expectations and then the expectations others put on us, too, were so high that you were always more focused on winning a championship than winning a Heisman."

It's a sentiment that Bradford—who reached the title game in his winning season—and Ingram—whose Crimson Tide claimed a championship the same year he took the trophy—could certainly have related to in playing for glamour programs Oklahoma and Alabama. But injury kept the second and third sophomores to take the Heisman from ever even presenting a challenge in their encores.

The setup for the 2009 race was unlike anything in the trophy's seventy-five-year history. Never before had a season begun with two returning winners, which this one had in Bradford and Tebow, and with Texas's Colt McCoy also back, it was the first time the top three vote-getters were all still in the college ranks.

"Just to win one is tremendously challenging," Bradford told the *Tulsa World*. "To win two is extremely hard to describe."

Especially when you consider that star-laden field. Bradford, though, was on his way to a strong start to his follow-up campaign as he rewrote the Sooners' record book in the season-opener against BYU at Dallas Cowboys Stadium.

Bradford hit Brandon Caleb for an 18-yard completion late in the second half to break Jason White's school record of 7,922 yards. But a play later, his bid for a second Heisman came to a screeching halt as he was hit by the Cougars' Coleby Clawson.

The linebacker broke through an offensive line that was playing with four new starters and drove Bradford into the turf, with the Sooner landing on his right shoulder. He was left writhing in pain, clutching his arm as he rolled around. The quarterback held his right shoulder as he walked off the field and a short time later was on the sideline in a T-shirt, his throwing arm in a sling and an ice pack on his shoulder.

Bradford had suffered a grade 2 or 3 AC joint sprain, and No. 3 Oklahoma absorbed a 14–13 loss that dropped it to 13th in the AP poll. The reigning Heisman winner wouldn't need surgery but would miss upwards of four weeks.

He received well-wishes from McCoy and Tebow, the former coming via a text message, as they grew close during the '09 trophy festivities and while rooming together at the Manning Passing Academy the summer before the '10 season.

"I told him I'd be praying for him and hope that he gets better soon," McCoy told ESPN.com. "I wish him the speediest recovery possible."

Added Tebow, "He came back for his [junior] year to do some great things, so I wish that he could come back and play it, too."

A month later—and with Oklahoma at 2–2 after routs of Idaho State and Tulsa and a 21–20 loss to Miami—Bradford did return to throw for 389 yards in a 33–7 victory over Baylor. However, a week later in the Red River Rivalry, Texas cornerback Aaron Williams went unblocked on the Sooners' second series of the game and dragged down Bradford as he tried to get away from the defender. Bradford landed on that same shoulder, re-aggravating the injury.

"It's extremely frustrating, obviously," Bradford said that day. "That's the way this season's gone for me. I missed three games, come out to start this one, and hurt my shoulder. It's really hard to put into words the frustration I feel right now."

A week later, Oklahoma announced that Bradford would have season-ending surgery to repair the joint and return it to normal strength, and twenty-four hours after that, the redshirt junior stood at a podium and in an emotional press conference, and said he was leaving early for the NFL.

"I dreamed about coming here," said Bradford, who was flanked by a number of his teammates. "The first time I got hurt, I was sitting on the sidelines knowing I was coming back—that was the light at the end of the tunnel. But to make this decision and realize I've played my last game at Oklahoma, it's really tough."

He had sought out the advice of the New York Giants' Eli Manning and San Francisco 49ers' Alex Smith, both of whom had suffered similar injuries, and felt that surgery and the pros were the right call.

"I talked with as many people as I could to make the right decision," Bradford said. "After talking to a lot of people, it seemed like this was the unanimous decision that everyone came to."

Bradford became the first returning winner since Navy's Roger Staubach in 1964—who himself suffered through an injury-plagued season—to not finish in the top 10 in voting.

That same fate would await Ingram, though unlike Bradford, there was no televised moment where his season crumbled before a nation's eyes.

****

Five days before the defending national champion Crimson Tide were to open the 2010 season against San Jose State, Ingram jogged off the practice field. For the most part, his teammates never even realized anything was wrong.

"He just said his knee was hurting a little bit," Ingram's backup, Trent Richardson, told the *Mobile Press-Register*. "He got off the field real quick. We didn't think it was that bad, and it's really not that bad anyway."

But it would require arthroscopic surgery, which a day later coach Nick Saban addressed in a statement.

"Mark will definitely be out for this week's game against San Jose State and we will manage this on a week to week basis beyond this week," Saban said. "We will make every decision in the future based on what's best for Mark and his career as we consult with [team doctors James Andrews and Lyle Cain] on his progress. This is not an injury that will affect Mark's future ability to make a full recovery in a relatively short time frame."

An expected two-to-four-week timetable meant Ingram would assuredly miss the opener, as well as the September 11 game against Penn State, and any real chance of another shot at the trophy.

To Ingram's credit, he didn't waste any time when he finally did get on the field September 18 at Duke, going around the right side of the line in ripping off a 48-yard dash on the first play of the game. He added runs of 50 and 20 yards en route to 151 yards and 2 scores on 9 carries.

"I just really wanted to make an impact right off the jump," Ingram told reporters. "It was very satisfying knowing we got the call and I was one on one with the corner and had to make the play. It was good to just set the tone early."

Ingram added 157 yards and 2 more trips to the end zone the following game against Arkansas in the SEC opener, but those would be his only 100-yard games of the season as his backup, Richardson, made the case for more carries.

Saban has more often than not relied on a two-back system in his time at Alabama, but it's been those rare occasions where one has demanded 45 percent or more of the team's carries that the Tide have been a force in the Heisman race. It happened in '09, when Ingram was responsible for 45 percent (249 of 550 at the time of voting) and went on to win the award; in '11 as Richardson had 263 of 473 (55 percent) and became a finalist; and in '15 with Derrick Henry, who had 60.4 percent of the attempts (339 of 561). Those backs also fueled the offense in three out of four of Saban's national title seasons.

But with Richardson running for a 204 combined yards in the first two games sans Ingram, it largely reverted into the typical Saban time-share. Ingram had 158 carries to Richardson's 112, and once again, a returning winner didn't crack the top 10.

That hadn't happened in back-to-back repeat attempts in forty-six years, since Vic Janowicz ('51) and Staubach ('64).

2013: Johnny Manziel, 2014: Jameis Winston

Integrity is right there in the Heisman Trust's mission statement—the first sentence, no less—charging that its honoree "best exhibits the pursuit of excellence with integrity."

Morality was trotted out in 1972 with Nebraska's Johnny Rodgers. At seventeen, he was part of a service station holdup that netted $90, and got off with probation and the suspension of his license. Later, he was picked up for suspicion of possessing marijuana, and ran a stop sign with a suspended license.

Morality was again a rallying cry by those who opposed Auburn's Cam Newton on his way to winning in 2010, after he faced allegations that his father, Cecil, and former Mississippi State player Kenny Rogers had sought $120,000–$180,000 from the Bulldogs during the quarterback's recruitment out of junior college.

Johnny Manziel was silenced for most of his history-making, trophy-winning season of 2012, though that was per coach Kevin Sumlin's policy of not allowing freshmen to give media interviews.

But he more than made up for it in his first offseason in the spotlight, with trips to Las Vegas and the NBA Finals. He partied with rappers Rick Ross and Drake and became friends with LeBron James and threw out the first pitch at Padres and Rangers games.

Johnny Manziel was the first redshirt freshman to win the award in 2012, but the Texas A&M quarterback finished fifth in his follow-up season. *(By Shutterbug459)*

Days before the SEC Media Days, Manziel departed the Manning quarterback camp, in what he said was a mutual decision after he overslept and missed activities.

"I don't feel like I've done anything that's catastrophic," Manziel said before a throng of reporters in Hoover, Alabama, at the SEC's preseason circus. "Of course, I've made my mistakes. It's time to grow up."

But then he became the focus of an NCAA investigation, as the day before the Aggies' preseason camp began it was reported that he was paid for thousands of autographs by brokers in Connecticut, Florida, and Texas.

"If the media did their research on who this kid was, no one would be surprised," 1998 Heisman winner Ricky Williams told the AP. "It's unfortunate, it's not his fault. It's who he's always been. Just because you won a trophy doesn't mean you're going to change your behavior."

Texas A&M and the NCAA could find no evidence that Manziel had received any money, but he had been found in violation of NCAA bylaw 12.5.1.2, which per the Division I manual states that: *After becoming a student-athlete, an individual shall not be eligible for participation in intercollegiate athletics if the individual: (a) Accepts any remuneration for or permits the use of his or her name or picture to advertise, recommend or promote directly the sale or use of a commercial product or service of any kind; or (b) Receives remuneration for endorsing a commercial product or service through the individual's use of such product or service.*

He was suspended for the first half of the season opener against Rice. When he finally did play, he took a hit from the Owls' Nick Elder on a scramble, jumped up, and made a hand gesture toward the linebacker, as if he was signing an autograph in thin air. Then, after throwing his first touchdowns pass, a 23-yarder to Mike Evans, Manziel threw the investigation in the face of the NCAA by rubbing his fingers together to symbolize money.

Those who had grown tired of his antics had their soapbox, and despite an even better redshirt sophomore season as a passer—3,732 yards and 27 touchdowns when ballots were due, compared to 3,419 and 24 scores in '12—he finished a distant fifth in the Heisman pecking order. A 1,501-point win for Florida State redshirt freshman Jameis Winston was the second-largest for any vote with a returning winner, and Manziel's place tied Tebow for the worst finish of any trophy-holder who had been invited to the ceremony.

Manziel later revealed his vote, and even he didn't top his own ballot. He went with Winston, followed by Boston College's Andre Williams, and himself in third.

The Texas A&M lightning rod at least made it back to New York as a finalist before leaving College Station for the pros, something Winston couldn't replicate in an equally rocky follow-up season.

****

For the record, the normal price for a cluster of snow crab legs at grocery chain Publix runs around $9.99–$11.99 a pound. It's a hefty figure for a college student, and when Jameis Winston left a Tallahassee store in April 2014 without paying for $32.72 worth, the Florida State quarterback provided social media with fodder for weeks.

Some of the most popular memes were of Winston from the Seminoles' BCS title game celebration, the crystal football trophy replaced by crab legs; the quarterback stiff-arming a defender wearing a Publix apron while he cradled the crustacean, the two superimposed onto a backdrop of the store; and a promo poster for Discovery Channel's *Deadliest Catch*, with Winston's head put onto a fisherman's body.

He was also issued an adult civil citation and forced to pay restitution and perform twenty hours of community service. It didn't impact his standing with the football team, as Winston—who also played baseball for Florida State—was suspended for a three-game baseball series, then reinstated.

"I went to the supermarket with the intent to purchase dinner but made a terrible mistake for which I'm taking full responsibility," Winston said in a statement. "In a moment of youthful ignorance, I walked out of the store without paying for one of my items."

But that incident wasn't the beginning, nor was it the end.

Winston claimed the 2013 Heisman over Alabama's A. J. McCarron despite a sexual assault scandal that, while not resulting in any charges, included admitted missteps by Tallahassee police. Thirteen percent of voters didn't include Winston on their ballot despite his guiding the Seminoles to an unbeaten regular season, and an eventual national title.

He was undeniably the year's most outstanding player and was awarded as such, even if some abstained from supporting him. Though the crab legs incident resulted in a tangible penalty, but not one that had an impact on football, a mid-September 2014 outburst in which Winston allegedly stood on a table in the student union and repeatedly shouted an obscene sexual phrase certainly did.

The quarterback was initially suspended for the first half of top-ranked Florida State's game against No. 24 Clemson, a ban that was extended after administrators found that Winston was not entirely truthful with them.

The Seminoles won 23–17 with backup Sean Maguire filling in, and when Winston returned, they continued a run toward another perfect regular season. But the quarterback was nowhere near as effective, with fewer yards (3,559 compared to 3,820 in '13), a worse completion percentage (65.3 after 67.9 the year before), fewer touchdown passes (24 in '14; 40 in '13), and more interceptions (17) than any other passer from a Power 5 conference.

In the summer of 2013, before he had seized the starting job, Winston joked with reporters when the topic turned toward dealing with the spotlight and criticism, "If I ever get Manziel disease, I want all of you to smack me in the head with your microphones."

Voters did so through their ballots. Winston had the worst finish of any reigning winner who didn't miss games due to injury, receiving just four first-place votes and 51 points overall, to come in sixth. A month later, he declared for the NFL draft.

Nine have come close, and nine have failed to stand alongside Griffin. So he waits, a place in history he never imagined he'd hold alone for quite this long.

"I thought several people could get it," he said. "More recently Tim Tebow when they started giving it to sophomores and they started giving it to freshmen. I thought there were plenty of opportunities for someone to do it twice and I thought that would be done."

CHAPTER FIVE
THE GREATEST RACE

THE T-SHIRT WAS the work of Norfolk, Virginia, entrepreneurs Dave Bushnell and Fred Kirsch, a simple design with an image of Georgia's Herschel Walker striking the iconic Heisman Trophy pose. Underneath the running back, it said "Who Else?"

Who else?

Answering that question can serve as rationalization as to how Walker had been denied the award as a freshman in 1980. Despite rushing for 1,616 yards and 15 touchdowns and leading the Bulldogs to a national championship, *Who else?* was a case study in the most notorious instance of voters being unwilling to get behind a player because of his age.

For all his brilliance, Walker came in third at 445 points behind the winner, South Carolina running back George Rogers, and trailed Pitt defensive end Hugh Green by 178. The sense around Athens, Georgia—and subsequently the whole of the college football universe—was that *Who else?* could no longer be an excuse for an exercise in ageism. Even if he was still eyeing a trophy breakthrough as a sophomore, Walker was the unequivocal focal point of the defending champs and a consensus All-American.

A season later, *Who else?* now mocked a system, and attempted to size up the contenders across the entirety of the game's landscape—a defiant declaration that was emblazoned on a cotton banner.

"You just know that he's going to be better than he was as a freshman, because of the obvious that you're more comfortable in the system, we're probably going to throw it to him a little bit," said Georgia quarterback Buck Belue. "That was the expectation, that we were going to do the back-to-back thing and he was going to lead the way.

"They didn't give it to him as a freshman, but we expected him to get it as a sophomore."

And how could they not?

The snub storyline of his freshman year only grew after Walker's 150 yards against Notre Dame in the 1981 Sugar Bowl, a performance that came with a dislocated shoulder and a yardage that was 30 more than the rest of his team accounted for.

Walker had already reached a different kind of celebrity status, receiving three write-in votes for president of the United States in the 1980 returns of Green County, Georgia, and his draw reached the Great White North as well, as Nelson Skalbania, the owner of the Canadian Football League's Montreal Alouettes, offered Walker a reported $2 million deal. "The negotiations got real serious," Walker told United Press International, "and it was 50–50 for a while."

His family backed up his future earnings by taking out a Lloyd's of London insurance policy—which was initially reported by the *Atlanta Journal* to be worth $1 million, but later dwindled down to below $200,000—that created enough of a hoopla that it necessitated his releasing a statement through the school's sports information office.

"My family felt it would be in my best interest to look into an insurance policy," Walker said. "I discussed it with them a great deal. I feel it is basically a private matter as long as it is within the rules and should be kept within our family."

It was within the rules, as it was Walker and not Georgia, meeting the insurance premiums—which were believed to be between $5,000–$7,000—through a deal with a bank that would defer payments until he turned pro.

"I was looking at him, and I said to myself, 'You're looking at a million dollars,'" Bulldogs fullback Ronnie Stewart told the *New York*

Times in 1981 of that initial report of the policy's worth. "He's just a man, just like me. But he's worth a million dollars."

At Georgia's picture day a month before the season, some 5,000 gathered for photos and autographs from the returning members of the national champs, and the throng had Walker sitting in full gear on a smoldering southern summer day for three solid hours. Of the seemingly grueling day, Walker—who also had designs on running in the 1984 Los Angeles Olympics and was working toward a black belt in karate—played it off as another part of his physical regimen. "[It's] a good workout in my writing," he told the *Rome News-Tribune*. "It has to stay in shape, too."

He was, without question, the game's biggest star, and stood as the presumptive preseason favorite to win the Heisman—even if he had no interest in discussing it before the season began.

"I don't think anyone can think about the Heisman right now," he told reporters that August. "You have to do your talking on the field."

Still, there were three other players who finished in the top 10 in voting in 1980 back on their respective campuses, and that group had combined for 52 first-place votes, fewer than half of what Walker registered (107). That included the nation's leading passer in BYU's Jim McMahon (fifth), Ohio State quarterback Art Schlichter (sixth, and who had been fourth in '79), and Michigan wide receiver Anthony Carter (tenth), and while they were known commodities, if momentum was setting the stage, Walker appeared to have it in excess.

"I felt like if anybody would break that [age] barrier that was unwritten about winning a Heisman, Herschel was one that was in a position to win it," said Bulldogs coach Vince Dooley.

The question with Walker at that time wasn't whether he was going to win *a Heisman*. It was about *Heismans*, and whether he could not only equal Archie Griffin as the only two-time recipient, but maybe even pass the Ohio State great.

"When you started to appreciate his talent and skill, you thought this could have been a multiple [-time winner]," said Belue, who played with Walker in both '80 and '81.

Hence the fearlessness—even if it was only for the sake of those try-ing to hock a product—to proclaim/dare/taunt, *Who else?* at pollsters to start a season in which the Bulldogs were replacing both of their starting offensive tackles and their right guard. But it would end up being *Who else?* that gave this dash to New York its bite, as a group of frequent archetypes fueled what remains arguably the greatest race in the Heisman's storied history.

The 1981 race would pit against each other the preseason favorite and youth, both embodied by Walker; the statistical monster in the form of USC's Marcus Allen; Pitt's Dan Marino as the face of the title contender; BYU's Jim McMahon, representing the challenger outside the power structure; and Schlichter, the presumed savior of an institu-tion of a program (and the starter since his freshman year), who had yet to deliver.

But what truly helps define the significance of this race is the immense confidence of those around Walker and those who faced him. As Tennessee coach Johnny Majors said that November, "Herschel Walker is the greatest player in America." And yet someone other than Walker was handed the trophy that year. Again.

There would be no fodder for the tin-foil-hat crowd this time, though. As Dooley says looking back on what would unfold that fall, "That's just the way things happen sometimes. It's all about timing, I guess."

****

Marcus Allen was on the floor, rolling around with laughter. "Say what?" he told *Sports Illustrated* for its preview issue. "The Heisman. Come on."

Humility was among the traits that defined Allen, the future Pro Football Hall of Famer, and there was maybe a twinge of that ahead of his senior season. But, in reality, the Southern Californian likely had his reasons for not buying in.

His Trojans career, to that point, had an always-a-bridesmaid vibe to it.

Recruited out of San Diego's Lincoln High—where he primarily played quarterback—he had joined the Trojans as a defensive back. They were already stacked there, boasting All-Americans Ronnie Lott and Dennis Smith, along with Jeff Fisher, so on the fourth day of practice in 1978, coach John Robinson moved Allen to tailback. He rode the bench, rushing 31 times for 171 yards and a touchdown for the Coaches' Poll national champions.

"They just said they thought I was a good athlete and they felt I'd fit in somewhere," Allen told the AP in '81 of his recruitment.

Another spring and another position change followed, this one completely unexpected: fullback.

Allen broke his nose on the first day of spring practice, and at 6-foot-2, 202 pounds, was giving up 30 pounds to the linebackers he was now attempting to block. But he proved an effective caddy for '79 Heisman winner Charles White, who would run for 1,859 yards and 13 scores.

"Marcus had never been asked to be a blocking back before, and I'm sure it was difficult for him," Robinson said in December 1981. "But he was enthusiastic about it and responded well."

Allen would finally get his chance at tailback as a junior, but the narrative surrounding the Trojans was that they were scrambling. They had a five-man battle at quarterback to fill Paul McDonald's shoes, with only two of them having accrued any previous playing time; All-American offensive guard Brad Budde was gone—oh, and they were replacing White with their fullback.

Robinson, though, knew the potential Allen represented.

"I'm convinced Allen will develop into one of the great backs in the country," he said that preseason.

Allen rushed for 132 yards and a touchdown in the Trojans' season-opening win against Tennessee and had three 200-yard games, including 216 against both Minnesota and Washington. Only Gamecocks Heisman winner George Rogers would run for more yards than Allen's

1,563 on 354 carries in '80, but that wasn't enough in the land of trophy winners, a field that included White, O. J. Simpson, and Mike Garrett and runner-up Ricky Bell. Midway through that season, the *Los Angeles Times* ran a headline asking "Does USC Finally Have An Average Tailback?"

"Accepting the tailback legacy at USC is a major adjustment," Allen told the Associated Press. "I've accepted it."

With the criticism came rumblings that he might not be suited to fill one of the game's most glamorous positions, and even his own coach's defense of Allen's numbers could come off as a backhanded compliment. But, in terms of the Heisman, Robinson was on board—even if Allen publically scoffed at it—especially after his tailback opened his senior year with 210 yards on 22 carries against Tennessee and a career-high 274 on 40 attempts against Indiana.

"Marcus has neither the flash of Charles White or the dash of O. J. Simpson, but he churned out 1,563 yards and 14 touchdowns in just 10 games [in '80] and is a definite Heisman Trophy candidate," John Robinson said ahead of USC's September 26 game against No. 14 Oklahoma, which followed those victories over the Volunteers and Hoosiers. Allen rushed for 208 yards and a pair of touchdowns in the Trojans' 28–24 win.

No longer the bridesmaid, he had now taken on the role of the tone-setter, and while Walker countered with 161 yards and a touchdown on 30 tries in beating those same Vols to open Georgia's season, and another 167 on 35 carries a week later on Cal, the Bulldog suffered the first setback. In a 13–3 defeat at the hands of Clemson on September 19, Walker fumbled 3 times and lost 2—including 1 on the Tigers' 17-yard line early in the game—and was limited to 111 yards on 28 attempts. It snapped Georgia's 15-game winning streak, dating back to the next-to-last game of the 1979 season.

Walker had captivated during his record-breaking freshman year, but Dooley saw something different when he took the field as a sophomore. The element of surprise was gone, and after averaging

5.9 yards per carry in 1980, Walker was managing 4.7 a try through three games.

"He shocked a lot of people as a freshman, because they were not ready for him or did not focus on him as a freshman as they did as a sophomore," Dooley said. "But some of the greatest runs he ever had were as a sophomore and they weren't the long runs. They might have been 10-, 12- to 15-yard runs that were just really classical runs, getting every yard that he can, whereas as a freshman, he would break [free], and if he broke, with his speed . . . people were surprised and the defenses were not ready as they were when he was a sophomore because they were focused on stopping him."

Walker was far from out of the race, though Allen was well on his way to laying claim to having the best chance at being the ninth straight running back to claim the Heisman. Beginning with Penn State's John Cappelletti in 1973, followed by Archie Griffin's two wins, Pitt's Tony Dorsett, Texas's Earl Campbell, Oklahoma's Billy Sims, White, and Rogers, it was the Age of the Running Back in the annals of the Heisman. Despite his initial take on his candidacy in the days before the season, Allen smiled when pressed as to whether he'd given any thoughts to winning.

"I'd love to win the Heisman," he said.

A quarterback hadn't received the trophy since Auburn's Pat Sullivan did so in 1971, though three would make a serious push to counter Allen and Walker, headlined by a passer fighting to get respect for his program, and his mind-boggling numbers.

****

"It was," Jim McMahon so profoundly stated, "a miracle."

Considered one of the greatest comebacks in bowl history, McMahon's summarization stuck, as what became known as the Miracle Bowl could also have served as a four-minute ad for the validation of McMahon and BYU. The quarterback had orchestrated a rally from down 20 to lift the Cougars to a 46–45 victory over No. 19 Southern Methodist, producing three scores in the final 2:33 of the 1980 contest.

"He was very good," said Cougars coach LaVell Edwards. "He had just an unbelievable last game as a junior to win that bowl game."

Down 6 points with 18 seconds left and the ball on the Mustangs' 41-yard line, McMahon missed on his first two pass attempts. Then, the Cougars went to what McMahon called the "save-the-game play."

The receivers went deep and everyone else stayed in pass protection, trying to give the quarterback as much time as they could offer. As the Cougars wideouts moved toward the middle of the field, tight end Clay Brown followed, all abiding by instructions that McMahon would throw it up and hope for a pass interference call.

Brown and SMU's West Hopkins went up for the ball, but it went right through the defensive back's hands. A collection of four defenders fell on the Cougars tight end, trying to wrestle the ball away, but as the referee surveyed the situation he signaled for a touchdown and one Mustang simply fell to his knees in the end zone in disbelief.

"It was a 'Hail Mary' pass," Brown said after the game. Qualifying his heroics at a Mormon institution, he added, "I can call it that because Jim and me are Catholics."

McMahon finished with 446 yards and 4 touchdowns on 32 of 49 passing, the punctuation mark on a season in which he set 26 NCAA records with 4,571 yards, 4,627 total yards, 47 touchdowns through the air and 53 in all, and a 176.9 efficiency rating. Those figures led all passers, yet it was Purdue's Mark Herrmann—whose stat line included 1,359 fewer yards, 24 fewer touchdowns, and whose rating was nearly 26 points behind McMahon's—that was the consensus All-American and was fourth in the Heisman voting with 405 points to McMahon's 189.

The Cougars rose as high as 12th in the AP Top 25 and finished 14th following the bowl victory, but the schedule and perception did the BYU passer no favors. Despite winning 12 games for the first time in school history, McMahon and Co. didn't face a ranked team until the postseason, and the team they lost to—New Mexico, by a 25–21 score in the opener—ended up 4–7.

BYU had made strides under Edwards. Behind a pass-happy offense that produced the nation's seventh-best scoring offense in '77 (37.9) and first in '79 (39.5), the Cougars had rattled off three straight nine-win seasons before going 11–1 in '79, but they had just one win over a ranked team in that span, topping No. 14 Texas A&M 18–17 in 1978.

"I think it would have been very difficult for [McMahon] to win it, looking back at it, just because of where we were from, and our lack of so-called competition that people were always talking about, too," Edwards said.

BYU quarterbacks had led the nation in passing yards in 1976, with Gifford Nielsen's 3,401, and in '79, as Marc Wilson threw for 3,720. But McMahon was different, Edwards notes, and no by-product of a system.

"What he had, just an uncanny, innate feel for throwing the football. In other words: getting it up on time," the coach said. "One of the biggest things you're always talking about is getting the ball up on time, throwing it on time, and the receiver makes the cut and the ball should be coming. This anticipation . . . this feel of not only where to throw it, but when. You don't talk so much about the when, but it's every bit as equally important as knowing where to throw it."

McMahon had that, the cachet of the Holiday Bowl triumph, and the Cougars garnered some respect with their highest preseason ranking ever at 16th in the AP poll. The quarterback got off to a fast start, throwing for 403 yards and zero scores and had games of 226 yards and 4 scores (Air Force) and 267 yards and 4 touchdowns (UTEP) before his season and his campaign were derailed in Boulder, Colorado.

"He wasn't ever really very big," Edwards said. "He was probably 180 pounds when he was throwing and he was about 5-foot-11, maybe six feet. So he wasn't a very strongly built guy. But he was very resilient. He took some pretty good hits and came right back up and was very,

very competitive that way. The big thing we wanted was to keep him healthy so we could get the season out of him."

McMahon was on track for a monster day against Colorado, completing 15 of his first 30 passes for 263 yards and 3 touchdowns, and added two more NCAA records to the thirty-five already on his résumé. But then came a hit by blitzing Buffaloes safety Ellis Wood with 13:41 left in the third quarter, which knocked the quarterback out of a game BYU would win 41–20. McMahon had suffered a hyperextended left knee and would undergo arthroscopic surgery that kept him out the next two weeks, games in which the Cougars edged Utah State 32–26 and fell to UNLV 45–41, as future Pro Football Hall of Famer Steve Young played in McMahon's place.

Even with that missed time, McMahon still led all Division I QBs with 272 completions, a 64.3 completion rate, and 155.0 rating, and racked up 2,395 yards and 15 scores in six games after his return. That was topped by throwing 7 touchdown passes against Colorado State—to go along with 538 yards—and he burned rival Utah for 565 yards in the season finale.

"I missed two ballgames [with a hyperextended knee] and that hurt my chances," McMahon told reporters. "But that's life."

The injury was a virtual death knell, even if he had rebounded to finish with 3,555 yards and 30 scores. While he was unable to overcome that blow to his campaign, another quarterback discovered just how devastating a late loss could be.

The 1980 Pitt Panthers were star-studded. The defense, headlined by Hugh Green, included five linemen who would all play in the NFL—Green, Rickey Jackson, Jerry Boyarsky, Greg Meisner, and Bill Neill—as did the offensive line of Jimbo Covert, Truss Grimm, Rob Fada, Mark May, and Ron Sams; receivers Dwight Collins and Julius Dawkins; fullback Randy McMillan; and kicker Dave Trout.

So deep was that roster that five non-starters went on to become NFL starters.

But it was sophomore Dan Marino who became the most accomplished of them all at the next level, and one of the best passers in pro history. Yet amid the '80 season, he was part of a quasi-quarterback controversy in the Steel City.

The Parade All-American's mere signing with his hometown Panthers in February 1979 was met with speculation of what it would mean for incumbent quarterback Rick Trocano, who months before Marino made his intentions known, had thrown for 1,648 yards and 5 touchdowns to 14 picks in helping Pitt to an 8–4 record and a loss to North Carolina State in the Tangerine Bowl.

"Competition in sports is everything," Marino told reporters at a press conference in the library of Pittsburgh's Central Catholic High School. "It should help Rick and me. Coach [Jackie] Sherrill told me he will never put me in until he feels I'm ready to play . . . I wouldn't want to play until I'm ready, either."

Seven games in, their hands were forced as Trocano went down against No. 17 Navy with a pulled hamstring, and Marino coolly responded with 227 yards and 2 touchdowns on 22 of 30 passing in a 24–7 win. The torch was seemingly passed, as Marino set a Panthers freshman record with 1,680 yards in an 11–1 season, and Trocano asked to be moved to free safety for his senior season, on the condition that he could still take over at quarterback if need be.

Pitt opened the season at No. 3 in the AP poll, but delivered two shaky offensive performances. It beat Boston College 14–6 despite Marino going 23 of 43 for 221 yards in his first 5-interception game on any level. "Everybody's going to throw interceptions," Marino told the *Pittsburgh Post-Gazette*. "Kenny Stabler threw five against the Steelers." The quarterback also grappled with a 35-mph wind in Lawrence, Kansas, which resulted in his hitting only 17 of 18 passes for 250 yards in topping Kansas 18–3.

A week later against Temple, Marino connected on 9 of his 15 attempts for 150 yards and 3 touchdowns before suffering a knee injury and giving way to Trocano, who directed a 55-yard touchdown drive in the 36–2 win. While Marino was back at quarterback and Trocano again in the defensive backfield the next two games—at Maryland, a 38–9 rout, and at No. 11 Florida State, a 36–22 loss, Pitt's only one of the year—Marino's knee injury resurfaced in the Backyard Brawl at West Virginia.

Trocano stepped in and led Pitt to a 4-touchdown second quarter in a 42–14 rout and would start the next four games before Marino made another appearance. Even when the sophomore did return, it was a time-share, with Trocano bringing the running threat to Marino's big right arm.

In a 45–7 dismantling of Army, the duo combined for a school-record 436 passing yards, and Marino's 20 completions were one more than Army even attempted.

"We're a strong, two-quarterback team," Trocano said after a 14–9 victory over Penn State in the regular-season finale. "It's hard for an opposing team to prepare for us. They never know who's going to be in there."

Trocano was again at the controls in the win over South Carolina in the Gator Bowl, running for one TD and throwing for another as he hit on 10 of 21 passes for 155 yards. Marino also delivered a touchdown pass, but he was just 7 of 13 for 78 yards.

There were plenty of unknowns going into 1981, as the Panthers had to replace nineteen players who had inked pro contracts and had just five seniors from that team that finished second in the rankings. "I should have gone with them," Sherrill quipped to reporters that pre-season of the personnel losses. In addition, the defense was decimated, with nine new faces.

"We're a long ways from having the football team we had last year," Sherrill said. "But unless we have some bad injuries, I don't think we'll dip too far."

The Panthers still began the year ranked eighth, largely because of the expectations for Marino.

Even though he missed four games, Marino still threw for 15 touchdowns—tied for 15th in the nation with seven others, including the Buckeyes' Schlichter—and 1,609 yards as a sophomore, and the thought of what he could do in a full season as a starter throwing to sophomore wide receiver Dwight Collins (10 touchdown catches in '80) enticed.

Marino eased in with 204 yards and 2 touchdowns in an opening 26–6 win over Illinois, then tossed 5 scoring strikes in a 38–7 rout of Cincinnati before throwing for a Pitt-record 6 touchdowns and 346 yards on 24 of 39 passing to sink South Carolina 42–28 in Columbia. But he suffered a badly bruised upper right arm against the Gamecocks and was forced to sit out the October 10 game with rival West Virginia, a 17–0 win in which the Panthers didn't gain a single yard through the air. Backup Dan Daniels attempted just 6 passes, one of which was intercepted.

Marino was back the following week, throwing for 3 touchdowns and 251 yards in a 42–14 blitzing of No. 11 Florida State, a game in which the quarterback would become the school's all-time leading passer.

Like McMahon, that missed game was devastating to his building campaign. But unlike the BYU star, Marino was playing at a national powerhouse, one that thanks to No. 1 Penn State's 17–14 loss to unranked Miami on October 26, went into the final month of the season atop the polls.

The Panthers cruised through Rutgers 47–3. Marino's line in that game: 18 of 28 for 239 yards and 3 TDs and one rushing score. They beat Army 48–0 (he played just three quarters, going 19 of 29 for 282 yards and 4 touchdowns) and Temple 35–0, a game in which Marino delivered 4 touchdowns and 249 yards on 20 of 34 passing.

Marino stood as the nation's most efficient passer behind 32 touchdowns, 2,348 yards, and a 60.5 completion percentage, and going into the regular-season finale against Penn State, coach Joe Paterno doled out his praise.

"Dan Marino has picked apart every defense he's seen," Paterno told *Field News Service*. "We're not going to stop him. We're just hoping for a couple of dropped passes, a couple of penalties, things like that."

Marino, though, seemed taken aback when told of the coach's comments, saying, "Coach Paterno is trying to blow my mind a little bit."

Paterno's remarks seemed almost prophetic— *"We're not going to stop him"*—as Marino hit Collins for touchdowns of 28 and 9 yards, respectively, in the opening 10 minutes to stake a 14–0 lead. But Marino would be picked off by Roger Jackson in the end zone on the first play of the second quarter, marking the first of his 4 picks in the game and 7 Pitt turnovers as the Panthers fell 48–14.

"Momentum is like a locomotive and when it got turned around we couldn't stop it," Sherrill told reporters.

The momentum of the Panthers' title chase was over as they tumbled to 10th in the AP Top 25, and so were Marino's Heisman hopes. But he had another season to live up to the expectations, saying that winter he believed he had "a good shot next year."

While that local product still had time, it was running out for Art Schlichter to meet the immense hype that followed him to Ohio State.

Had he lived a couple hours closer to Penn State, the Bloomington, Ohio, native would admit at the end of his junior season, "I probably would have ended up there."

Schlichter was heavily recruited by the Nittany Lions, but when he announced in 1978 that he was sticking close to home, he did so with a statement that would have seemed like blasphemy for much of coach Woody Hayes's twenty-year tenure.

"Coach Hayes has assured me that Ohio State intends to build more passing into its offensive attack," Schlichter said. "He and [assistant] coach [George] Chaump have told me the Ohio State offense will be retailored to challenge a quarterback to use all his abilities."

This quarterback was that special, having not lost since he was in fifth grade and throwing for 1,794 yards and 21 touchdowns and running for 7.4 yards per carry for Miami Trace High School. Hayes, he of the three-yards-and-a-cloud-of-dust mindset, would be changing his ways as Chaump, who is credited for recruiting Schlichter, succeeded in getting the old man to get with the times.

"How soon will he start? That depends on several things," Hayes told reporters upon landing Schlichter.

They removed one of those obstacles, shifting all-Big Ten quarterback Rod Gerald to receiver to make way for the freshman.

It had been 10 years since the Buckeyes won their last consensus national championship, and Schlichter arrived as the next Ohio native that would be the savior of a program that is a state's lifeblood.

He started from Day 1, throwing 5 interceptions in a 19–0 loss to Penn State, but by the end of the 1978 regular season had racked up 1,250 yards on 87 of 175 passing with 4 touchdowns and ran for 590 yards on 157 carries with 13 scores. Still, the inability of the rest of the offense to catch up in a new era of Buckeyes football was glaring, as he also threw 21 interceptions.

If picks started the narrative of his first year in Columbus, it was only fitting one ended it—the final interception Schlichter threw that year led to one of the most infamous moments in college football history, and the downfall of a legend.

Facing third-and-five on the Clemson 24-yard line with 1:59 left in the Gator Bowl, Schlichter dropped back and threw a short pass into the middle, but Tigers middle guard Charlie Bauman stepped in front of it and pulled down the pick. Bauman was run out of bounds toward the Ohio State sideline and tackled by Schlichter near the feet of Hayes. As the Tiger rose, Hayes pulled him by the back of his jersey toward him and swung his right arm at Bauman's throat.

At age sixty-five, after 321 games, the fourth-most wins in history at 238, two national titles, thirteen Big Ten crowns, three Heismans, and a pair of National Coach of the Year awards, Hayes's illustrious career came to an unceremonious end. He was fired as the Buckeyes flew home from Jacksonville.

In stepped Earle Bruce in Hayes's place and he hired Schlichter's high school coach, Fred Zechman, as quarterbacks coach and put an even greater focus on the passing attack, often using all five receivers on a number of plays. It resulted in Schlichter standing as the nation's top-rated passer midway through a season in which he passed for 1,816 yards and 14 scores; he also ran for another 430 yards and 9 touchdowns, and he cut down the interceptions in dramatic fashion, tossing just 6 with a 145.9 passer rating that was fifth-best in the country.

Schlichter finished fourth in the Heisman voting behind Charles White, Billy Sims, and Marc Wilson, all seniors. In fact, he was the only player in the top six that would be returning the next fall.

Add in the fact that he and the Buckeyes were two points from a perfect season, losing 17–16 to USC in the Rose Bowl, and began 1980 atop both the AP and UPI polls, and Schlichter was dubbed the favorite in the trophy chase. The stage was set for the junior passer to live up to the hoopla that followed him to Ohio State.

Said Syracuse coach Frank Maloney ahead of their meeting in the season opener, "He's the best quarterback in the country."

Schlichter's stats were strong, as he was 122 of 226 through the air for 1,930 yards and 15 touchdowns, compared to 9 picks and he rushed for 325 yards and 7 touchdowns, and claimed the program's career total offense crown with a season remaining. None of that, though, could mask the fact that the Buckeyes as a team fell flat.

They played on two nationally-televised ABC games and dropped both of them, losing to No. 11 UCLA 17–0 on September 29, and against archrival Michigan 9–3 to end the regular season. A spot in the Fiesta Bowl opposite 10th-ranked Penn State followed, and Ohio State was dumped 31–19 to end the year at 9–3.

Schlichter didn't even end up being the Heisman leader at his own position within his own conference, as Purdue's Mark Herrmann was fourth to Schlichter's sixth. He drew eighteen first-place votes, and 158 points in all.

"It was a major disappointment because we had great expectations," Schlichter told UPI the summer of 1981. "I don't even like to talk about it."

As Schlichter's backup, Bob Atha, told *Sports Illustrated*, "They built up Art [for the Heisman] and it hurt him very much. And I think Art was conscious of it to a point that he ran the options in a way to protect himself from injury. You can't blame him. We're friends, but I felt sorry for him."

During the winter of his junior year, the addiction that would ultimately be Schlichter's downfall began to dig its claws into him. He had begun gambling, his first big win coming close to April 1979 when he put $72 down on a trifecta at Columbus's Scioto Downs race track and won around $400. Two years later, he was gambling on sports and recounted to *People* how he had lost more than $5,000 in one weekend betting on baseball.

"When you lose, you face a down period," he told the magazine for its January 15, 1996 issue. "Then the disease starts talking to you, telling you the next bet will be better than the last one, the next bet will put you where you want to be."

The No. 4 pick by the Colts in the 1982 draft, he would lose his entire $350,000 signing bonus betting over a seven-week period. After losing nearly $500,000 on basketball games, his bookies threatened to expose him, and Schlichter went to the FBI and the NFL. Reinstated in '84, he continued gambling and would be released five games into '85 when the Colts discovered he'd been betting during his ban.

Schlichter signed with the Bills as a free agent for '86 but lasted one preseason game, and a year later was arrested by Indianapolis police and charged with betting $232,255 on MLB, college, and pro football games.

He was relegated to signing with the CFL's Ottawa Rough Riders and then the Arena Football League, where he ended his football career in 1992.

In 2012, at age fifty-two, he was sentenced to eleven years in prison for scamming participants in a sports ticket scheme in which he promised tickets to college and NFL games, tickets that, despite receiving thousands of dollars in payments, were never delivered. He was also ordered to pay $2.2 million in restitution.

"Schlichter instead spent the money on personal expenses, gambled with it, or used it to repay older debts," federal prosecutors said in a statement.

He is scheduled to be released in 2022.

Those problems were still hidden from the public in 1981, as Schlichter entered his final season at the helm of the Buckeyes offense, and much like his entire time in Columbus—and what would follow—nothing went according to plan.

Ohio State claimed its first three games, victories over Duke, Michigan State, and Stanford—the latter of which came in a duel with John Elway in which Schlichter passed for 240 yards and 2 scores to Elway's 248 and 2 touchdowns—but dropped three of the next six games to tumble to 18th going into the regular-season finale vs. seventh-ranked Michigan.

Schlichter had his moments amid the losses, setting a school record with 458 passing yards in a 36–27 loss to unranked Florida State on October 3, and when he left the penultimate game against Northwestern, a 70–6 rout, the quarterback received a standing ovation from the Ohio Stadium crowd.

He put on a show in his final meeting with the Wolverines, marching the Buckeyes 82 and 80 yards for touchdowns and rushing for a pair of touchdowns, with the game-winner coming on a 6-yard sweep with 2:50 remaining in a 14–9 win. Schlichter passed for 131 yards and ran for 9 more, the finishing touches on a season with 2,551 yards passing and 17 touchdowns and another 6 scores on the ground.

There would be no Rose Bowl, though, as Ohio State could only earn a share of the Big Ten crown with Iowa at 6–2. The schools never met on the field to create natural separation, but the Buckeyes had been to Pasadena in 1980 and the Hawkeyes last made it in 1959, so Iowa got the invitation to face Washington.

Schlichter and the Buckeyes were instead off to Memphis to face Navy in the Liberty Bowl, a game they'd win 31–28. The three losses hurt his Heisman chances, as did expectations that followed him over four years as a starter—and the quarterback seemed resigned to it in the days before the announcement.

"I won't be disappointed if I don't," Schlichter told UPI of winning the trophy. "I'd love to win it, but if I don't, I don't. A lot of people don't even get considered for it and I'm fortunate enough to have been."

In another season, any of those quarterbacks could have won, but they had worked their ways out of the race, by what could be chalked up as an ill-timed loss, the perception of playing a lesser level of competition, or the backlash of impossible hype.

But in reality, it was just a matter of two of the greatest running backs in the college game's history making a push for the 47th Heisman their own duel.

****

Marcus Allen considers himself a goal-oriented person. So when he told USC offensive coordinator John Jackson in the summer of 1981 of the number on which he was fixated for his senior season, Allen did so firmly believing it could be done. Never mind that no one had ever hit that figure before.

Two thousand yards.

The single-season NCAA record belonged to Pitt's Tony Dorsett, who ran for 1,948 on 338 carries during his Heisman-winning season of 1976. But the way Allen figured it, if he had gained over 1,500 yards in his first season at any level with consistent carries at tailback, then 2,000 wasn't out of the question.

"After understanding everything, the light went off and I said, 'I got it,'" Allen told the website The Postgame in 2015. "I came back and told my coach 'I want to gain 2,000 yards.'

"I figured if I gained 1,500 yards and I didn't know what I was doing . . . now, I know what I'm doing."

Through five games, Allen had piled up 1,136 yards—an average of 227.2 per game—and wouldn't rush for less than 150 until October 24, when Notre Dame "held" him to 147 and a touchdown on 33 carries in the Trojans' 14–7 victory. The following week, Allen ran for a career-high 289 yards and 3 touchdowns against Washington State, and then had 243 more with 3 more scores against Cal to break Dorsett's single-season record.

What the Panthers running back did in 11 games, Allen needed just nine to accomplish, pushing his season total to 1,968 with two games to play.

"I'm still not that concerned about records, only getting to the Rose Bowl," Allen said after beating the Golden Bears. "But when the season is over, I'll probably look back and say 'Wow.'"

He'd have to settle for 2,000 yards instead of a trip to Pasadena.

Standing 32 yards shy of his preseason goal against seventh-ranked Washington, Allen reached it on his fourth carry, on which he went 13 yards before linebacker Ken Driscoll brought him down. But afterward, Allen was more concerned with the Trojans having lost 13–3, giving them another Pac-10 defeat after falling 13–10 to Arizona on October 10. USC's Rose Bowl hopes weren't completely dead, but they would need to beat UCLA the following week and hope that Washington and Washington State played to a tie.

"I broke the [2,000-yard] barrier in the first quarter, but I wasn't thinking about that," Allen said days later, "[I] was only thinking about the game and the outcome. It was a day to remember and a day to forget."

It was also a day with which Walker was generally unimpressed. While Allen was making history, the Georgia running back ran for 165 yards and a touchdown in a 24–13 victory over Auburn. That gave him 1,667 yards on the season, 51 more than he had during his record freshman season, and he still had a game to play.

"I don't think stats matter," Walker said after the win.

But if it was stats voters wanted, Walker supplied it in the regular-season finale against Georgia Tech, torching the in-state rival for 225 yards and four touchdowns in a 44–7 rout. Meanwhile, Allen had 219 yards and a pair of scores, the second of which came with 2:14 to play, as the Trojans edged UCLA 22–21.

Allen stood at 2,342 yards and 22 touchdowns going into the voting; Walker had 1,891 yards and 18 scores. The Trojans were 9–2 and eighth in the AP Top 25 behind their tailback and headed to the Fiesta Bowl and a date with No. 7 Penn State; Georgia was 11–1, ranked second, and set to face No. 10 Pitt in the Sugar Bowl.

"[The trophy] should go to the best athlete and the athlete who helps his team the most," Walker said as their duel reached its final days. "He has a lot of yards, but so do I. As far as who is the best running back, I think I am a whole lot better."

McMahon, conceding that he was out of the running the day before the announcement, believed that in delivering the unprecedented, Allen should win out.

"I've seen Marcus play and along with Herschel Walker, they've made a name for themselves," McMahon would say. "Marcus had a really good year, and if I was to pick, I'd say he was the leading candidate right now."

Voters agreed, as Allen received 441 of the first-place votes and 1,797 points in all, 598 points ahead of Walker—who topped 152 ballots—while McMahon was third, Marino fourth, and Schlichter fifth.

"I have found my place in history as the best player in the country at this particular time," he said after his selection. "I put in a lot of hard work, but I was not alone. My parents, my coaches, and my teammates all are responsible for this award. . . . At the risk of sounding self-centered, I would have voted for myself."

The margin of victory was no landslide in terms of point differential, with 14 votes decided by a bigger gap, but Allen had received 57 percent of all possible points. Only six winners had drawn more at that point in time: O. J. Simpson (80.6 percent in 1968); Tony Dorsett (74.9 in 76); Gary Beban (63.5 in '67); Richard Kazmaier (60 in '51); Archie Griffin (59.5 in '74); and Jim Plunkett (58.7 in '70).

"To tell you the truth, I thought the voting would be a lot closer," Allen said days later at the All-American weekend. "I would never let myself believe that I could run away with it like I did."

He wasn't alone in that thinking, as Walker—who disclosed that he felt his sophomore status and needing to live up to the impact of his first season "ruined whatever chance I had"—said, "I don't know what else I could have done this year. Maybe I have to gain 3,000 yards."

Back in Athens, they understood. There was simply no arguing with history. Allen had delivered the greatest single season of any college running back, going over 200 yards five straight times and seven in all. Walker had no answer for that unparalleled number: 2,000.

"Was I disappointed? Well, yeah, a little bit," Belue says now. "You always want your guy to capture stuff like that and it was a little disappointing because we expected him to follow that freshman year up and you wouldn't have those people voting against him just because he was a freshman.

"He had just an unbelievable season, Herschel did, as a sophomore, but Marcus was so amazing, I don't think anybody thought that he got cheated."

Walker's moment finally came a year later, the junior rushing for 1,752 yards and 16 touchdowns. He dominated the voting, with 525 first-place votes in distancing himself from Stanford's John Elway by 695 points. But even then, when his pupil's Heisman moment seemed assured, Dooley admitted he still wondered if Walker would be denied one more time.

"You could not help but get anxious about it until it was finalized and you knew it was the way that it turned out," Dooley said. "But I really felt like he was going to win, but until it actually happened, there's no question that you get a little bit nervous about it."

Like those T-shirts, he couldn't help but have it rattling around his head: *Who else?*

CHAPTER SIX

HEISMAN HINDSIGHT: HOW WOULD BOWLS CHANGE VOTING?

ESPN'S TELECAST CUT back to the field, where at the center of Stanford's celebration following its 45–16 drubbing of No. 5 Iowa in the 2016 Rose Bowl, reporter Maria Taylor awaited Cardinal running back Christian McCaffrey. A fan with an agenda was also present, attempting to get in on the conversation.

"How aware were you of your production throughout the game?" Taylor asked McCaffrey, while the fan—a man wearing a Stanford hat and shirt—positioned himself squarely behind player and media member, so that he was in full view of the camera.

"Not at all, really," McCaffrey replied. "When you're playing, the game goes by so fast and you just focus on the next play.

"And I think that's why our team is successful," he continued, "because we're not worried about what's happening in the now. We're worried about the next play and what we can do to help the team be successful."

As McCaffrey got near the end of that answer, the fan fidgeted. He held up his index finger, and for a brief moment, looked as though he had lost his nerve. His mouth opened as if he was going to yell something, and maybe thought better of it.

His stat line was staggering. McCaffrey scored a 75-yard touchdown on the first play from scrimmage in racking up 139 all-purpose yards in the first quarter alone, and 48 seconds into the second quarter, he ripped off a 63-yard punt return for a score.

It was arguably the masterpiece of what had been a record-breaking sophomore season. In all, McCaffrey ran for 172 yards on 18 carries (9.6 per carry), had 4 receptions for 105 yards (98 of which came after the catch) and a score and another 91 yards on returns. Those 368 all-purpose yards smashed the old Rose Bowl mark of 346 by Wisconsin wide receiver Jared Abbrederis in the 2012 edition against Oregon, and were the fourth-highest total in any bowl game.

Nearly a month before at the Heisman Trophy ceremony, McCaffrey was already the single-season all-purpose yardage king. He had ripped that record away from 1988 winner Barry Sanders when the Stanford running back amassed 461 yards against USC—the fifth highest single game total in history—in the Pac-12 Championship Game. That exploitation of the Hawkeyes defense simply pushed his yardage to 3,864, which was 614 more than that of Sanders, and still 338 ahead if you count Oklahoma State's bowl game, which in '88 the NCAA didn't add to season statistics.

Second in the voting to Alabama's Derrick Henry at 293 points back, this stood as a statement in every sense of the word—even if the Stanford back didn't want to be the one to verbally deliver it.

But then it happened. He held both of his hands to his mouth and blurted it out.

"HEIIISSMANNNN!"

He wasn't done. Taylor asked McCaffrey about the Cardinal's focus going into the game, and the man, becoming emboldened and amused with himself as he smiled at the crowd of media that was gathering, shouted it twice.

"HEIIISSMANNNN! . . . HEIIISSMANNNN!"

When the topic turned to motivation of finishing behind Henry in the Heisman race, the man took a shot at the winner, referencing his yardage in eventual national champion Alabama's 38–0 rout of Michigan State in the Cotton Bowl the day before, and was sure to put McCaffrey's historical season into context.

"75 YARDS . . . DERRICK HENRY!"

"BETTER THAN BARRY!"

McCaffrey, who made it seem as if he was unaware of the fan's antics, smiled at the Sanders comment. Then, the fan tapped into the thinking of many who watched this piece of history unfold.

"RE-VOTE!" he yelled. "RE-VOTE!"

Obnoxious as he may have been—and WWE icon "Stone Cold" Steve Austin may have summed up social media's reaction when he tweeted, "Would someone from ESPN shut the dipshit up while Christian McCaffrey does a postgame interview?"—he brought up a point that remains one of the more perplexing ones when it comes to the Heisman Trophy.

Why isn't the voting held after the bowl games have been played?

For much of the award's history, it made sense. While the NCAA began keeping stats in 1937, there were few bowls, and the reporting on figures from those games was sketchy. The games just didn't matter, basically standing as exhibitions. Until 1968—with the exception of 1965—the Associated Press crowned its national champion at the end of the regular season.

The bowls now had a direct impact on the course of the season, but the Heisman still had its reason for sticking to its normal timetable. Statistics accrued in the postseason were not included in yearly totals, meaning Iowa's Chuck Long throwing for a then-record 6 touchdown passes in the 1984 Freedom Bowl (that mark was pushed to 7 in 2014 by Central Michigan's Cooper Rush), Sanders's aforementioned yardage in the '88 Holiday Bowl, or Ty Detmer's 594 yards in the '89 edition of that game (a record that still stands) shouldn't be factors.

But that changed in 2002 when, based on a survey of Division I, II, and III sports information directors, the NCAA opted to begin including those postseason stats as part of the season totals. It wasn't a vast majority, though, as according to the governing body, Division I-A—the sub sector that accounts for the major programs—sports information directors voted 42–37 in favor, but the question was posed to just 79 of the 117 Division I-A schools.

The decision wasn't retroactive, though, meaning no one would be going back and including those pre-2002 performances. As Jim Wright, the NCAA's director of statistics, told *The Oklahoman* in 2011 regarding that decision, when another of Sanders's records, 39 touchdowns in a season, was being challenged, and would ultimately be tied by Wisconsin's Montee Ball, "We did not have the resources to, literally, recreate every bowl game with complete stats and play-by-plays that would allow us to see what additional records would be impacted."

Whether or not you buy that argument, the fact of the matter is that bowls matter in every facet of college football—except when it comes to the Heisman. Still, as Heisman Trust president William J. Dockery said, there are no plans among the nine-person committee to force the award to alter course.

"People suggest it. People criticize . . . you're going to be criticized no matter what you do," he said. "No, the award traditionally has been for the outstanding college football player during the season. So with the playoffs, there have been suggestions that it should be changed, but I think virtually everyone is happy with the way it works presently.

"Otherwise you're talking about one game or two games, rather than a season dictating [the winner]."

Which brings us back to McCaffrey and his hype man—no, not the fan, but rather Stanford coach David Shaw.

"I think he was the best player in America before this game, so I think it's just the icing on the cake for us," Shaw said in the postgame press conference. "I do think it's a shame that a lot of people didn't get a chance to see him during the course of the year. Apparently the games were too late.

"But the bottom line for me is his heart, and his determination is evident in every single practice and every single game. Christian, I told him at the Heisman ceremony and I told him again not too long after that, we need him to lead, and he's leading by example and showing guys how to work and push themselves because that's what great players do."

Likely to Shaw's dismay, many still didn't tune in to see McCaffrey and the Cardinal, with the Rose Bowl drawing a 7.9 television rating, the lowest on record for the event since 1983. But it was still an all-time performance in one of sports' marquee events against a team that, up until the final week of the regular season, was making a case for a spot in the College Football Playoff.

McCaffrey's record day—along with the outings of the other two players who joined him in the Heisman ceremony—certainly could have made the vote even more interesting.

The stage on which he picked to deliver it could have been better, but the obnoxious Stanford fan was right: Henry was limited to 75 yards against Michigan State, though he had two touchdowns, and followed that with 158 yards and 3 scores on 36 attempts—putting him over 2,000 yards on the season—against Clemson in the national championship game.

Opposite Henry was Tigers quarterback Deshaun Watson, who, after throwing for 187 yards and running for a season-high 147 against Oklahoma in the Orange Bowl, threw for 405 yards and 4 scores to go along with 73 rushing yards vs. the Crimson Tide.

The 478 total yards bested Vince Young's 467 in 2005 for the most in a title game.

Those yards through the air were the third-most that one of Nick Saban's Alabama defenses had ever given up, and he became the first quarterback in Division I history with 4,000 yards passing and 1,000 yards rushing in a season.

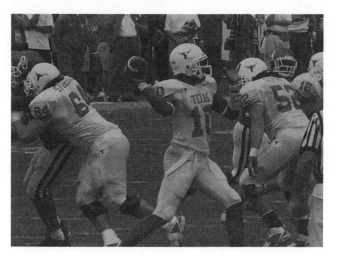

Texas's Vince Young, the 2005 runner-up, had 467 total yards in beating USC in the national title game, but would it have been enough to supplant runaway Heisman winner Reggie Bush? *(frankielon/Flickr)*

We could have had history vs. history vs. a 2,200-yard rusher for the Heisman. Ultimately, Henry may have still won out as the backbone of Alabama's title run, even if some had walked away believing that he had been individually upstaged by Watson.

Regardless of the outcome, it would have been riveting.

But while that race could have been further amplified by including bowl games, there is an inherent risk involved: eliciting knee-jerk reactions.

Young was sensational in giving Texas the 2005 national title, the lasting image coming on the final play, facing fourth and five, as the quarterback scrambled untouched for an 8-yard touchdown with 19 seconds remaining. The Longhorns had taken down seemingly unbeatable USC and its Heisman winners, Reggie Bush and Matt Leinart.

Think that would have been enough to sway the vote?

It certainly could have saved the Heisman Trust the trouble of vacating that year's trophy, but it would have been wrong.

Bush was the most electrifying player of that season, and he was every bit as Heisman-worthy against Texas with 279 total yards, with

82 rushing, 95 receiving, and 102 on kick returns. Young delivered a transcendent performance, but he had received just 79 first-place votes to Bush's 784, and while the margin of victory may have become smaller, to think that he could have made up that kind of ground had the voting come a month later may be unrealistic.

Revisionist history does have its place, though. There are instances prior to 1968—that year when bowls started to truly hold significance in the national landscape—where the trophy could have changed hands if the postseason was taken into consideration, namely 1964, when Tulsa's Jerry Rhome could have supplanted winner John Huarte of Notre Dame, who didn't play in a bowl, while Rhome led the Golden Hurricane to a victory over Ole Miss, and '67, as O. J. Simpson lost the award to UCLA's Gary Beban, but burned Indiana for 128 yards and 2 touchdowns on 25 carries in USC's Rose Bowl win (Beban—who threw just 8 touchdowns on the season, along with 8 interceptions—and the Bruins weren't part of that postseason).

But the years since the AP's inclusion of bowls have seen ten occasions where a delay in voting may have made a difference, and it could have helped to settle one of the most contentious finishes the Heisman has ever seen.

NOTE: Missing from those races that could have changed: 1980. While Herschel Walker was again spectacular in rushing for 150 yards and 2 touchdowns in a win over Notre Dame that gave Georgia a national title, and George Rogers was held in check in South Carolina's loss to Pitt and fumbled twice, nothing about the voters of the time tell us they would have been any more interested in voting for a freshman. Plus, Rogers did finish with 113 yards, so it wasn't as if he was entirely a non-factor.

1971: Ed Marinaro over Pat Sullivan

He was the NCAA career record holder with 4,715 yards, capped it off with a national-best 1,881 yards in his final season, and would go on to win UPI Player of the Year.

Yet, Cornell tailback Ed Marinaro would lose the Heisman by 152 points to Auburn quarterback Pat Sullivan, and when he appeared on a pre-taped ABC Sports special that aired three days after the announcement, he didn't hide his resentment.

"I should have won it, not him," Marinaro said.

Sullivan's classmates took a step to make him feel better, with a second-place trophy displayed at J&M Bookstore on the Auburn campus for several weeks, including a plaque that read:

2nd Place Heisman Trophy

Presented To

ED MARINARO

WHO THINKS HE'S THE BEST ANYWAY

FROM THE STUDENTS

OF

AUBURN UNIVERSITY

1971

But Marinaro may have received the real thing had the vote been delayed.

Three days after receiving the Heisman, Sullivan had his worst game of the season, as the fifth-ranked Tigers fell 31–7 to No. 3 Alabama, a loss in which the quarterback threw for a season-low 121 yards on 14 of 27 passing with 2 interceptions. It was following that loss that ABC aired Marinaro's remarks.

"As for that show on nationwide television after the Alabama-Auburn game . . . I had the opportunity to express myself in that I had come in second in the balloting," Marinaro told the Associated Press in April 1982. "But there's no way I could have known that Pat and Auburn were going to lose and he couldn't have an outstanding day. I felt sorry for Pat the way that turned out."

Cornell didn't reach the postseason in '71, but sitting at home could have simply strengthened Marinaro's case, as Sullivan followed that forgettable outing against the Crimson Tide with another opposite No. 2 Oklahoma in the Sugar Bowl.

Sullivan passed for 250 yards in a 40–22 loss, with 1 touchdown and an interception, and that lone score came with the Sooners up 40–14. Meanwhile, he was also upstaged by Oklahoma QB Jack Mildren, who after coming in sixth in the voting, had 30 rushes for 149 yards and 3 touchdowns and was named game MVP.

Mildren would have certainly seen a spike coming off that performance, and Sooners running back Greg Pruitt (95 yards and a touchdown) may have made a charge up from third in the voting, but Marinaro was positioned to take full advantage of Sullivan's missteps after he was given the award. He took three regions (East, Midwest, and Far West) to Sullivan's victories in the South and Southwest, and even if voters would have overlooked the Tigers quarterback's last two games, he was going to have even more difficulty taking the Southwest, where he had to contend with Pruitt and Mildren.

All that being said, there was one huge factor in the Heisman finish that Marinaro has gone back to that could have kept him from winning, regardless of what else transpired.

"I think it's legitimate to think that the Ivy League cost me the Heisman," he told the AP. "You can't tell me that any other player who set 12 NCAA records wouldn't have won it if he played somewhere else."

1990: Raghib Ismail over Ty Detmer

As detailed in previous chapters, Ty Detmer's setbacks after winning the trophy—hours after against Hawaii, in that season's bowl game vs. Texas A&M, and in three losses against ranked opponents to start his follow-up campaign—took the luster off his victory, and are arguably, years later, making it that much more difficult for contenders from outside the major conferences.

That's not all on Detmer, but had it been Notre Dame's Raghib "Rocket" Ismail that won instead, would it have changed the perception of candidates from smaller schools in the future?

The runner-up by 305 points, Ismail largely defined that season's Orange Bowl with what might have gone down as the Heisman Moment That Never Counted.

With 1:05 to go and Colorado up 10–9, Ismail fielded the punt at the 9-yard line and cut up the middle of the field, breaking through a group of four Buffaloes that converged on him, including Chad Brown, the linebacker rushing in from the All-American's left side. He made contact, but couldn't wrap Ismail up. As the Rocket broke toward the right sideline, Tim James—whose job was to provide outside containment—made a run at Ismail, falling forward as he reached out with both hands. But James came up empty, and Ismail outran both Colorado punter Tom Rouen and Ron Bradford—the latter had an angle on the return man, but he couldn't match his speed.

Ninety-one yards later, Ismail strolled into the back of the end zone and took a knee as if in prayer or exhaustion and was joined by teammate Rod Smith. The Irish defensive back pulled Ismail to his feet and hugged him, and a moment later, Ricky Waters jumped on them both, knocking them back to the ground. The three lay there celebrating, then slowly rose as the public address announcer boomed.

"THERE IS A FLAG ON THE FIELD."

"I remember taking that hit [from Brown] and thinking, *Hey, I'm still on my feet, just get outside,*" Ismail told *Sports Illustrated* in January 1991. "When I heard them announcing a penalty, I thought maybe it was defensive holding. Then I thought, *Yeah, right.*"

When James made his move toward Ismail, Notre Dame's Greg Davis hit him on the side, a clip that—while not blatant—would wind up costing Ismail and the Irish.

"I saw Rocket stumble, and I blocked him," Davis told the *New York Times*. "If he came through the hole clean, I wouldn't have had to block him."

The Buffaloes would hold on 10–9, and were left as split national champions, losing the UPI crown to Georgia Tech by a single point, while they won the AP title.

Running back Eric Bieniemy led all rushers in that Orange Bowl victory, but he had just 89 yards rushing and another 19 receiving. Finishing a distant third in that year's Heisman voting—he was 684 points behind Detmer and trailed Ismail by 379—it's difficult to believe he could have won. But Ismail?

Primarily a wide receiver with 33 catches for 699 yards and 2 scores, his true impact was in his all-around efforts, as he also ran for 537 yards and 3 touchdowns on 67 carries, returned 14 kicks for 336 yards and a score, and had 13 punt returns for 151 yards. He touched the ball 127 times in all and averaged 13.56 yards per carry.

Rocket managed 6 catches for 57 yards and ran 3 times for minus-1 yard in Miami, but don't think that the punt return against Colorado—nullified or not—along with the lure of his playing for Notre Dame wouldn't have won out after Detmer's setbacks.

1992: Garrison Hearst over Gino Torretta

Alabama had faced its share of Heisman winners before. It had seen Tim Brown (1987), Bo Jackson ('85), Doug Flutie ('84), Pat Sullivan ('71), and Frank Sinkwich ('42), but none of those meetings came with the player having already claimed the trophy.

Miami's Gino Torretta was the first, and in a clash of the nation's top two teams at the Sugar Bowl in 1993, the second-ranked Crimson Tide proceeded to make him look anything but outstanding.

"I knew they were good," Torretta said after a 34–13 loss that would be the Hurricanes' first game without an offensive touchdown in seven seasons and their worst loss in five years.

On the first play of the second half, Alabama cornerback Tommy Johnson picked off Torretta's offering and set up a short touchdown run by Derrick Lassic. After the ensuing kickoff, Torretta threw a first-down interception, this time snagged by George Teague, who ran it back 31 yards for another score.

The end result was two Alabama touchdowns in 16 seconds to claim a 27–6 lead.

"We faked blitzes and dropped two and three deep," Johnson told reporters. "I think we got into Torretta's head."

Torretta threw 3 picks in all—his second 3-interception outing over the course of three games, the last coming November 11 against No. 6 Syracuse—and completed just 42.8 percent of his passes (24 of 56).

"Gino did not play his best football game of the year. That's obvious," Miami coach Dennis Erickson said after the loss. "He made a couple of bad decisions. Those two scores were obviously the turning point."

Torretta being the choice of Heisman voters has always seemed to be a case of awarding him for Miami's dominance over his entire career. He was, after all, 26–1 as a starter before the Sugar Bowl, and already had two national titles on his résumé. In fact, he would remain the only two-time champ and Heisman winner until Matt Leinart, and later Tim Tebow, matched him, but his numbers were never all that flashy.

Torretta's 3,070 yards at the time of voting were sixth in Division I-A, and he was tied for tenth with 19 touchdowns. Houston's Jimmy Klingler claimed both of those statistical crowns, throwing for 758 more yards than the Hurricanes quarterback and 13 more scores. The only major national category in which Torretta finished higher than fifth was in total yards per play, at 6.98, which was tied for third.

He won as a leader, but if he was receiving the credit for Miami's successes, could he have taken the trophy after falling flat in the Sugar Bowl? Torretta still might have finished higher than runner-up Marshall Faulk (who didn't play in in the regular-season finale, a 63–17 Hurricanes romp that had been dubbed the Heisman Bowl), and whose San Diego State team didn't make a bowl game. Plus, he had that double stigma of being a sophomore and playing for an outlier school.

The opportunity would have been there for Georgia's Garrison Hearst. He finished third—sitting 418 points behind Torretta—and couldn't catch Faulk, who had 83 more rushing yards to lead the nation at 1,630, but Hearst ran for 163 yards and 2 touchdowns in a 21–14 Citrus Bowl victory over Ohio State, and had runs of 13, 11, and 8 in an 80-yard drive to set up the game-winning score.

There was enough of a backlash from Torretta's and Miami's performance that a Hearst victory would have been possible, even if it would have appeared to be a knee-jerk reaction.

1995: Tommie Frazier over Eddie George

The story goes that in 1991, Nebraska recruiter Kevin Steele sat down in a Palmetto, Florida, living room with a Manatee High School quarterback who had a very clear vision of his future:

Win a national championship (or two)

Be an All-American

Win the Heisman

"I felt that if I came here and played well, the way I'm capable of playing, then good things are going to happen," Tommie Frazier would tell the Sarasota *Herald-Tribune* four years later, as the Cornhuskers quarterback readied to attend the '95 Heisman Trophy ceremony.

Invited to New York along with Northwestern's Darnell Autry, Iowa State's Troy Davis, Ohio State's Eddie George, and Florida's Danny Wuerffel—a group that included the country's leaders in rushing attempts (Autry at 387), rushing yards (Davis with 2,010), rushing touchdowns/total yards from scrimmage (George's 24 and 2,344), and in touchdown passes/efficiency (Wuerffel at 35 and 178.4, respectively)—Frazier, who directed Nebraska to a third straight unbeaten regular season while throwing for 17 touchdowns and running for 14 in the option attack, knew where he stood in the pecking order.

"After looking at everything and everyone who is a contender, I feel I'm the best player out there," he said.

Frazier would have to settle for two of his three goals, failing in his trophy chase as he watched George win, totaling 1,460 points to Frazier's 1,196 behind 268 first-place votes to 218 for the Nebraska senior. Wuerffel finished third (987), with Autry fourth (535) and Davis fifth (402).

George was buoyed by a Buckeyes single-season rushing record, including a program-best 314 and 3 touchdowns in a November 11 dismantling of Illinois. But despite another 100-yard game from George in the Citrus Bowl—he had 101, to be exact, to go along with a score—Ohio State fell 20–14 to Tennessee. Volunteers running back Jay Graham outrushed George, totaling 154 yards and a touchdown.

Frazier countered with an epic performance against fellow Heisman finalist Wuerffel as the top-ranked Cornhuskers met No. 2 Florida in the Fiesta Bowl.

Frazier threw for 105 yards and a score and ran for another 199 and 2 touchdowns, as Nebraska rolled 62–24, delivering the second-worst rout in 30 meetings between the nation's top two teams, trailing only Army when it beat Notre Dame 48–0 in 1945.

For Frazier, the game was defined by one play, one simply known as The Run.

With the Cornhuskers facing second down on their own 25-yard line in the waning seconds of the third quarter, the quarterback ran the option right, faked the pitch, and gained 11 yards before he was met by a mass of five Gators defenders at the 36-yard line. He somehow emerged from the fracas, breaking 7 tackles and dragging two would-be tacklers for several yards before he was free, and headed to the side-line en route to a 75-yard touchdown and a 49–18 lead.

Said Florida coach Steve Spurrier afterward, "Tommie Frazier ran right through us."

The run was the longest scoring run in Fiesta Bowl history, the longest in Cornhuskers history, and helped Frazier set an NCAA record for the most rushing yards by a quarterback in the postseason.

Another championship in hand, Frazier said of his performance, "I had a great career at Nebraska. There's no better way to end it."

With The Run, George's setback, and Wuerffel being picked off three times and sacked a career-high seven (once for a safety), Frazier may have capped that career by crossing one more item off that to-do list he rattled off before he even arrived in Lincoln.

1997: Woodson Still Beats Manning

Delaying the voting until after the bowls are complete isn't always a matter of rewriting Heisman history. In this case, it's about performances that could have helped to strengthen an argument.

As broken down in Chapter Three, there was a perception—especially in Knoxville, Tennessee—that ESPN was pushing Michigan's Charles Woodson over Tennessee's Peyton Manning, as the Wolverines defensive back became the first primarily defensive player to win the trophy.

With the two going on to illustrious NFL careers that, interestingly enough, both ended in 2016, they remained linked because of the Heisman and their cases for it.

Woodson impacted the game in so many different facets, on defense, offense, and in the return game, but he couldn't match Manning's résumé after four years in Phillip Fulmer's program.

That final season, the Volunteers quarterback was selected as the SEC Championship Game Most Valuable Player, as well as the winner of the Davey O'Brien Award and the Johnny Unitas Trophy. He also held 42 program, conference, and NCAA records. Plus, he was the son of College Football Hall of Famer, Archie.

But the case for Manning would have been dealt a serious blow after Tennessee and No. 2 Nebraska played in the Orange Bowl that year.

The Cornhuskers came in 28th against the pass, giving up 183.9 yards per game, but the belief was Tennessee—sixth in passing at 331.8 ypg—could exploit it with Manning at the controls. Instead, he had just 134 yards and didn't complete a pass for more than 20 yards as the Volunteers went to a short passing game. He threw his lone touch-downs—a five-yarder to Peerless Price—with Nebraska already up 28–3.

"We didn't want to hold the ball very long," Manning said after the 42–17 loss. "There were probably a couple of times where we could have thrown the ball long and I didn't do it, but some games are like that."

The decision to not go deep—and give the Cornhuskers' defense shots at the quarterback—could have had something to do with him playing after rupturing a sac in his knee in the SEC title game that resulted in a six-day stint in the hospital before Christmas. Nevertheless, the result was Manning's second-lowest passing total of his final season.

Hours before the Tennessee quarterback's college finale, Woodson was shouting on the Rose Bowl sideline, "We did it baby. We did it. We did it."

With Washington State up a touchdown with eleven minutes left in the first half, the cornerback intercepted Ryan Leaf, who was third behind Woodson and Manning in the voting, stepping in front of receiver Kevin McKenzie to grab a poorly thrown ball.

"I pretty much knew what route [McKenzie] was going to run," Woodson told the *Baltimore Sun* afterward. "I cut in front of him and then Ryan Leaf threw kind of a wobbly pass at me."

He also made two key offensive plays with the Wolverines trying to drain the clock late in the game, catching two third-down passes in a 21–16 win to earn a share of the national title with Nebraska.

Woodson wasn't the game's MVP; that would be quarterback Brian Griese, who threw for 251 yards. But with a title and a strong final performance, could he have created an even bigger buffer with Manning in the Heisman vote? The bigger question may have been whether Leaf, after throwing for 331 yards and a score in the loss, would have challenged the Volunteers' quarterback for second.

Imagine that: Peyton Manning in third. There might have been an entirely new conspiracy theory, one stretching from Knoxville to Ann Arbor and Pullman.

2000: Josh Heupel over Chris Weinke

Much has been said—including in this book—about the factor that age can play in the voting, but Florida State's Chris Weinke faced it in a different way in 2000. After spending six years in the Toronto Blue Jays farm system, where, as a first baseman, third baseman, and outfielder, he hit 69 home runs and carried a .248 average in 716 games, Weinke enrolled in school in Tallahassee. He was twenty-four years old.

At twenty-eight, he led the Seminoles to their third national championship game in as many years, and became the oldest Heisman winner in history, leading the nation with 4,167 yards passing and 33 touchdowns to 11 interceptions.

But he was left off 122 ballots as he earned a 76-point win over Oklahoma's Josh Heupel, marking, what was at the time, the seventh-closest vote ever.

"Everything that's happened is because of the experience I've gained, not the age I've attained," Weinke said at the time. "When I went back to football at Florida State, I was no better a quarterback at twenty-four than I was at eighteen."

It's not as if he was the only one missing from voters' top three, with 106 ballots returned sans Heupel, who had 3,392 yards and 20 touchdowns to his credit. Weinke wound up with 369 first-place votes to Heupel's 286 (the Oklahoma passer led with 290 second-place nods), in giving the Seminoles a second Heisman (coincidentally, the first came via Charlie Ward in '93, who was part of the same recruiting class with Weinke out of high school). But would more voters have sided with Heupel after the Sooners beat Florida State 13–2 in the Orange Bowl?

Like in the previous two bowl meetings between players that finished 1–2 in the voting—Ohio State's Archie Griffin vs. USC's Anthony Davis in 1974 and South Carolina's George Rogers facing Pitt and Hugh Green in 1980—this was claimed by the runner-up.

Heupel was carried off the Pro Player Stadium field on his teammates' shoulders, telling reporters, "It doesn't get any sweeter than this, baby," after throwing for 214 yards and an interception. He didn't exactly steal the spotlight, but he helped generate just enough offense, running option plays and draws in a game defined by defense, which amounted to the lowest-scoring Orange Bowl since Penn State beat Missouri 10–3 in 1970.

"He took some vicious hits out there, vicious," Sooners offensive coordinator Mark Mangino told reporters. "He did what he had to do to win the game. That's why he's a winner.

"The bottom line is, he's a winner. He proved that. He's 13–0."

Weinke threw for 274 yards, but also tossed a pair of interceptions, including one in the end zone with 16 seconds left, as Florida State was limited to 301 yards, 248 under its season average.

"I wasn't hitting," Weinke said that night. "If the quarterback isn't throwing very well, you're not going to be successful. It was tough. It was frustrating after gaining so many yards all year."

With some voters already quietly protesting Weinke despite setting a single-season Seminoles passing record and leading them to the brink of a national title, it's very likely the door would have been open for Heupel, championship in hand.

2001: Dorsey or Grossman or Harrington over Crouch

No race could have potentially become more interesting with the inclusion of the bowls, if simply for the fact that the 2001 race may have ended up going in a number of different ways.

Voter response was the lightest in more than two decades, an aforementioned result of a delay in mail service after the terrorist attacks, even though the Downtown Athletic Club extended the deadline by a day and a half. That had the accounting firm of Deloitte & Touche LLP still receiving ballots hours before the announcement.

"Under the circumstances, I think it turned out pretty good," DAC president Jim Corcoran told the Associated Press.

If ever there was a year to ditch the show-must-go-on credo and move the presentation, this was it. But Eric Crouch would win in the fourth-closest vote—besting Florida's Rex Grossman by 62 points. Then he and Nebraska were subsequently railroaded by Miami 37–14 in the BCS Championship Game.

Crouch ran for 114 yards on 22 carries and lost a fumble, which led to Miami's first score. He passed for 62 yards and an interception, which resulted in another Hurricanes touchdown, as James Lewis returned it 42 yards for a pick six. The loss marked the first time Crouch was held without a touchdown since September 18, 1999, against Colorado.

"We turned the ball over, and that's what killed us," Crouch told reporters. "We knew Miami was that type of defense, they live off turnovers. We got down too far."

The stellar play of the Hurricane's Ken Dorsey—third in the voting—certainly played its part as well. The junior passed for 362 yards and 3 scores to cap a perfect season and improve to 26–1 as a starter.

That would have likely given him the Heisman in a post-bowl world, though Grossman was also sensational in Florida's 56–23 dismantling of Maryland in the Orange Bowl. He led the Gators to touchdowns on his first six drives and threw for 248 yards, even though he didn't enter the game until 6:03 into the second quarter for missing curfew.

"Six possessions, six touchdowns. That's unbelievable," Spurrier said in his postgame radio interview. "I don't think he threw a real bad pass the whole night."

Then there was Joey Harrington, his 350 yards and 4 passing touchdowns powering the Ducks to a 38–16 victory over Colorado—which came in with wins over No. 2 Nebraska and No. 3 Texas in consecutive weeks—in the Fiesta Bowl. Completed before Miami's rout, the game gave Oregon the hopes of a split national title if the Cornhuskers won, though the Ducks would instead have to settle on ending the season at No. 2 in the rankings.

"I'm really surprised how the game turned out," Harrington said then. "I always believed we were going to win. The way we did it kind of surprised me."

Where would voters have turned? Grossman, as a sophomore, would have been the unlikely choice six years before Tim Tebow broke through for the class, especially with him missing time due to a disciplinary reason (though would Spurrier have kept him out with a Heisman on the line?). In a Dorsey-Harrington debate, perfection is likely to have won out, putting the Miami quarterback at the podium.

As for Crouch, it's difficult to see him finishing higher than fourth after the Huskers' loss, a dramatic shift for a player who had more first- (162) and third-place (88) votes than anyone a month before.

2003: Eli Manning over Jason White

A Jason White win by one of the slightest of margins—128 points—over Pitt's Larry Fitzgerald seems like it could have been all the more unlikely after the Oklahoma quarterback completed just 13 of his 37 passes for 102 yards, tossed a pair of interceptions, and was sacked seven times in a 21–14 loss to LSU in the BCS title game.

"I said to him, 'Excuse me, Mr. Heisman. I'm going to be coming at you all night,'" said Tigers defensive end Marquise Hill after LSU limited the nation's No. 1 offense to a mere 154 yards. The Sooners came in averaging 461.4. "I think our conference [the SEC] is the hardest and Jason White wasn't anything we hadn't seen before."

The only touchdown he threw went LSU's way, as Marcus Spears picked off White's first pass of the second half and ran it back 20 yards for a touchdown and a 21–7 Tigers lead.

"This damaged [the year] quite a bit," White said after the Sooners ended their season at 12–1 and dropped to third in the AP and Coaches' Polls. "You win twelve games and that's extremely hard to do nowadays in college football, and now you don't have anything to show for it. That's disappointing."

As strong as Fitzgerald was that season, tying for the national lead with 22 touchdowns and 1,672 receiving yards—168 more than second-place Geoff McArthur of Cal—he wouldn't have been the clear winner after the postseason.

Fitzgerald all but disappeared in the Panthers' 23–16 loss to Virginia in the Continental Tire Bowl. He had 5 catches for 77 yards, ending his NCAA record streak of 18 straight games with a touchdown, and was targeted just six times the entire game. On Pitt's first possession, it had first-and-goal at the 1-yard line, and the Panthers went to their goal-line offense, which left Fitzgerald on the sideline as all four plays failed.

"I was definitely part of the game plan," Fitzgerald told reporters. "Virginia just did a terrific job of taking me out of the offense."

USC's Matt Leinart made his case, shredding Michigan's sixth-ranked pass defense for 327 yards while throwing 3 touchdowns and catching another on a 15-yard reverse handoff from Mike Williams, as the Trojans claimed the AP national title.

At sixth in the voting the month before with just five first-place votes and 127 points in all, the belief that Leinart could have risen up to win the Heisman even after the victory over the Wolverines may be a stretch.

Eli Manning, though, could have been in the right position with the right performance and the right lineage to take the trophy after his own playoff performance.

The Ole Miss quarterback was third with 710 points, but threw for 259 yards and 2 touchdowns and had a rushing score as the 16th-ranked Rebels beat No. 21 Oklahoma State in the Cotton Bowl. The victory gave Ole Miss its first 10-win season since 1971, and was the program's first triumph in January since the '70 Sugar Bowl.

The quarterback at the helm of the Rebels on that day in 1970? Eli's dad, Archie.

"When I came to Ole Miss, everyone expected me to bring the program back to its glory days," Eli said. "I didn't want to put that kind of pressure on myself."

The patriarch came in third in the '70 voting behind Stanford's Jim Plunkett and Notre Dame's Joe Theismann, and Eli's big brother Peyton, of course, was the runner-up in 1997. If the Cotton Bowl came into play, there's a real possibility that the youngest Manning—with his final performance, the missteps/underwhelming efforts of his challengers and the fact that he's a Manning—could have done what Archie and Peyton couldn't when it came to the Heisman.

2006: Darren McFadden over Troy Smith

"Not everything in life is going to go the exact way you want it," Troy Smith said after he and Ohio State, the nation's top-ranked team the entire season, had been shellacked 41–14 by No. 2 Florida in the 2007 BCS title game. "I don't have any regrets, though. I really don't. We came out and fought. We came up short.

"Sometimes you have great games and sometimes you don't."

That night would prove to alter the college football landscape, as the SEC took over, starting a streak of seven consecutive national titles. The game's place as a springboard, of course, wasn't clear on January 8, 2007. It was simply a stunning beatdown, as the Buckeyes—who were seven-point favorites and winners of 19 straight—fell to a Gators team that many felt didn't belong in Glendale, Arizona.

Ohio State managed just 82 yards, and its Heisman-winning quarterback, quite literally, took the brunt of the punishment.

The Heisman winner, after receiving 86.7 percent of the first-place votes (801), also tallied 91.63 percent of the possible points with 2,540—both records. Yet the lasting image of Smith in his final game was his being chased down by helmetless Gators linebacker Earl Everett. He was sacked five times in all, was just 4 of 14 passing for

35 yards and an interception, and was held to minus-29 rushing yards on 10 attempts.

Given this result, had the vote taken place after the title game, who would have been best positioned to take advantage?

Among the top five vote-getters, running back Darren McFadden (Arkansas), who was the runner-up, was held in check—compiling 89 yards on 19 carries—and out of the end zone in a 17–14 loss to Wisconsin in the Capital One Bowl. Third-place Brady Quinn completed just 15 of 35 passes for 149 yards and two picks in Notre Dame's 41–14 defeat at the hands of LSU in the Sugar Bowl. West Virginia's Steve Slaton (fourth) had 11 rushing yards on 3 carries and was outplayed by his quarterback, Pat White, who had 131 yards passing, 145 rushing, and 3 total touchdowns, in beating Georgia Tech 38–35 in the Gator Bowl. Finally, Michigan running back Mike Hart had only 47 yards on 17 carries in losing to USC 32–18.

Hawaii's Colt Brenann—sixth in the voting—had the most impressive bowl game, torching Arizona State for 559 yards, 5 touchdowns, and a pick on 33 of 42 passing in a 41–24 win in the Hawaii Bowl. That capped a record-setting season in which he led the nation in nine major statistical categories, including yards (5,549), touchdowns (58), efficiency rating (186), and completion percentage (72.6).

He would have remained a long shot, though, playing in the WAC with zero wins against Top 25 teams and only one against a major-conference opponent in Purdue, which was 8–6.

McFadden, despite those struggles against the Badgers, ran for 1,647 yards and 14 scores, had 149 yards and another touchdown receiving, reached the end zone in the return game, and threw for 3 more scores out of the Wild Hog formation during the regular season—the work of offensive coordinator and future Auburn coach Gus Malzahn. That dynamic game may have been enough, especially after Smith's debacle against the Gators.

2008: Tim Tebow over Sam Bradford

We already know that the majority of voters were prepared to make Tebow the equal of Archie Griffin in 2008, backing him with nine more first-place votes than the winner, Oklahoma's Sam Bradford, and thirty-four more than second-place Colt McCoy of Texas.

It wasn't enough, as he came in behind Bradford and McCoy, in what amounted to the second-closest gap between first and third in history at 151 points, trailing only 2001 when Dorsey was 142 shy of Crouch.

But after the bowls, it may have been even more difficult to deny the Florida quarterback a spot as the second two-time winner.

"Tebow," Gators receiver Percy Harvin said afterward, "just call him Superman."

Tebow overcame a career-high 2 interceptions, throwing for 231 yards and 2 touchdowns—the second of which, a four-yard jump pass to David Nelson with 3:07 to play, proved to be the clinching score—and ran for 109 yards. It was vintage Tebow with a dash of something very different as, after a 13-yard run, he was pulled down hard by the Sooners' Nic Harris. Tebow popped up and jawed at the defender, then did the Gator Chomp. The result was an unsportsmanlike conduct penalty.

"I was already motivated for a national championship game. But you know, there was some trash talking going on, and it just gets me going during the game," Tebow told reporters.

On the other side of the field, Bradford wasn't horrendous, throwing for 256 yards and 2 scores, but he also tossed a pair of interceptions, along with 15 incompletions on his 41 attempts. He was resigned to being a spectator as Florida, led by Tebow, claimed a second title.

Runner-up McCoy certainly would have put up a fight in post-bowl voting, after his late-game heroics against Ohio State in the Fiesta Bowl. Down 21–17 with 2:05 to play, the quarterback hit on 7 of 10 passes for 76 yards—including 3 big ones on fourth-and-3 when he hit James Kirkendoll—and ran for 2 more yards. It culminated with a 26-yard scoring strike to Quan Cosby with 16 seconds to play to give McCoy a school-record 41 completions, 414 yards, 2 passing touchdowns and another on the ground.

"He is so strong-willed and he is a guy that's very confident, and he never thinks he is going to lose," Texas coach Mack Brown would say.

McCoy may have been the choice, especially if some voters still refused to put Tebow in Griffin's class. But that seems the only scenario that would have kept Tim Tebow from history if the voting took place just a month later.

With forty-one bowl games being hosted as of the 2016–17 season, the Heisman's tradition of awarding the trophy prior to their start has become outdated. Of the 128 Football Bowl Subdivision teams, 63 percent are playing in those postseason games, and given that just one Heisman recipient to date has been on a losing team—Paul Hornung on 2–8 Notre Dame in 1956—the winner is a lock to be in one of those games.

It's not likely to change anytime soon, but for an award that has overcome so many biases and glass ceilings over the years, preserving the sanctity of the Heisman may need to include getting with the times.

CHAPTER SEVEN

O. J., BUSH, AND TARNISHED BRONZE

"**F**AME IS A vapor, popularity is an accident, and money takes wings," O. J. Simpson told *Sports Illustrated* in November 1979, a quote that he was unsure of the origins of, but had heard it one night on TV in Buffalo, the words bringing him out of his chair. "The only thing that endures is character."

The downfall of the former Southern California running back, beginning with him as the centerpiece of a shocking murder trial, stripped all that away from the 1968 Heisman Trophy recipient.

Quickly, fame turned into infamy.

On July 28, 1994, a month after the Bronco chase on Los Angeles's 405 Freeway, USC custodians noticed that the copy of Simpson's Heisman that was given to the school, along with his jersey from the '68 season, were missing from the lobby of Heritage Hall.

School spokesman Rob Asghar said in a press release that "the removal of the trophy and jersey is believed to be the first incident of vandalism or theft against memorabilia located in the building." But the student newspaper, the *Daily Trojan* reported in the spring of 1994 that women's basketball coach, Cheryl Miller, had stopped the theft of Charles White's jersey. White had won the Heisman in 1978.

This was different, though. People had flocked to the heart of the redbrick campus in the aftermath of Simpson's arrest on a double murder charge for killing his ex-wife, Nicole Brown Simpson, and friend

Ronald Goldman. When Simpson was leading police on that low-speed chase, the Los Angeles Police Department came to the football offices requesting that as a precautionary measure Simpson's items be removed, for fear that they would be stolen.

As the only staff member in the office, kicking coach Jeff Kearin obliged, taking the trophy and jersey out of the case and hiding them.

"It has nothing to do with shame," USC assistant Jeff Kearin told the Associated Press of the items' removal. "He's still a great Trojan and a great football player, a huge part of the heritage of USC football."

Three days later the items were back on display . . . until workers discovered the empty Plexiglas cases. The items had previously been sitting on top of podiums, which had since been dismantled and the items gone. Los Angeles police investigators—who believed two thieves were responsible—found that the screws that were holding the display together had been removed.

"They just lifted up the Plexiglass box that covered the trophy and took it, along with the jersey," Lt. James Kenady of USC security said to the *Los Angeles Times*.

USC sports information director Tim Tessalone told ESPN.com in 2009, "We waited for a while, hoping it might turn up. It never did. It's probably in the bottom of Santa Monica Bay. You can't fence a Heisman."

Another piece of Simpson's football legacy showed up on the side of Cleveland's Interstate 77 near the East 30th Street a year later. An Ohio Department of Transportation litter crew came across a nearly 40-pound bust that had been stolen from nearby Canton's Pro Football Hall of Fame in July 1995. The suspect, a white male estimated in his thirties, had taken it as crowds died down at the end of Hall of Fame Week.

That bust remains in the HOF, and in the wake of the trophy being stolen, the Trust would supply USC with another copy. USC continues to display it, along with those won by Mike Garrett (1965), Charles White (1979), Marcus Allen (1981), Carson Palmer

The copy of O.J. Simpson's Heisman, which replaced the one that was stolen from USC's Heritage Hall in 1994.
(Robert Raines/Flickr)

(2002), and Matt Leinart (2004)—but these days the school has increased security measures, as all of the Heisman cases are alarmed.

Simpson's trial gripped a nation and the verdict—an acquittal—divided it. The civil suit brought by Goldman's parents cost him his Heisman Trophy, as the former running back was forced to sell it to raise funds to pay the $33.5 million judgment. The award fetched $255,500 in auction in 1999, purchased by Tom Kriessman, the owner of a small steel company, who said he only bid to impress his then-girlfriend.

"You just get caught up in things sometimes," Kriessman told the *Washington Post* in 2013. "It sort of snowballed and it happened." He keeps the Heisman in a safety deposit box in Philadelphia, rarely visiting it.

Simpson is serving a nine- to thirty-three-year sentence in a Nevada prison for armed robbery and kidnapping stemming from a 2007 incident in the Las Vegas hotel room of collectors in which he demanded the return of memorabilia the ex-running back claimed were stolen.

His character—*the only thing that endures*—was tarnished long ago, but Simpson remains a recognized member of the Heisman fraternity, relaying his ballot from prison. In fact, Simpson's not alone in that arena, as 1959 winner Billy Cannon served two and a half years for his part in the seventh largest counterfeiting scheme in US history, but what he accomplished on the field remains untouchable.

During the court-ordered auction in 1999 to begin satisfying the wrongful death judgment against him, a conservative Christian group spent upward of $16,000 on Simpson's Hall of Fame plaque and signed USC and Buffalo Bills jerseys. The plaque—bought for $10,000—was dismantled and set on fire, the jerseys left smoldering.

"We are destroying O. J. Simpson's property in front of the L.A. courthouse because the criminal justice system is destroying justice before our very eyes," a Denver radio host, Bob Enyart, told the *Los Angeles Times*.

But as an onlooker screamed out: "You can't take it away from him! He still earned it!"

Therein lies the harsh reality of dividing O. J. Simpson, the man at the center of one of this country's most famous court cases, and the man known as "Juice." As far as the Heisman's keepers are concerned, any legal troubles have and will continue to have no impact on the player that the Trojans running back had been during his winning year of 1968.

"The rules are that the person has to be an eligible college athlete to win the trophy," said Heisman Trust president William J. Dockery. "What happens after they win the trophy is obviously concerning to the Trust, and would prefer that there are no bumps in the road, but we don't feel that we have any ability, once the trophy is earned by somebody legitimately, [to take it away].

"A certain segment of society makes mistakes, and probably the percentage of Heisman winners who have is probably less than the percentage of people in society who have gotten involved in things like O. J. got involved in."

When he accepted the trophy that season, Simpson detailed his conflicting feelings on being a football star, saying, "I'm here because I'm O. J. Simpson, football star, not because I'm just O. J. Simpson. I couldn't afford to be here any other way." Then he added something that would seem even more impossible decades later. "Sometimes," he said, "I just wish I could be a normal person again, to play football without having to share my life with the public."

A year after finishing second to rival UCLA's Gary Beban, he received 2,853 points—which, it should be noted, came when there were 1,200 registered voters, a figure that was later pared down—a total that is the most of anyone, and he still holds the record with 855 first-place votes. Even Ohio State's Troy Smith, who sat atop 91.6 percent of ballots, the most in history, didn't earn as many firsts (801) as Simpson did in that bloated voting environment.

Simpson remains a measuring stick for every vote, so while he may no longer have his Heisman, the Heisman—in every way that truly matters—still has him.

What it doesn't have is Reggie Bush.

In September 2010, the giant No. 5 jersey—Bush's number—that sat just to the right of Matt Leinart's in the peristyle end of the L.A. Memorial Coliseum was removed. These days, hashtags and asterisks have been added to dozens of mentions of his exploits in the Trojans' media guide, which is now littered with "Bush's records at USC have been vacated due to NCAA penalty," "Bush's participation later vacated due to NCAA penalty," and under the Heisman Salute portion of the 200-plus-page tomb, "USC TB Reggie Bush won 2005 Heisman Trophy, but award was later vacated due to NCAA penalty."

The exorcism of Bush from Trojans football lore was swift. Just three months removed from the NCAA handing down sanctions that were its toughest since Southern Methodist's football team was given the "death penalty" in 1986—its entire 1987 season was canceled and while it could have played an abbreviated schedule in '87, chose not to—USC followed the governing body's order to disassociate itself from Bush and former basketball player O. J. Mayo, both of whom were found to have received improper benefits.

The NCAA infractions committee's sixty-seven-page report stated that from October 2004 to November 2005, Bush, his mother Denise, and his stepfather LaMar Griffin joined sports marketers Lloyd Lake and Michael Michaels to form the agency New Era Sports and Entertainment. The company then provided Bush and members of his family a rent-free home in San Diego, airfare, and a vehicle. They also supplied Bush with the suit in which he accepted his Heisman Trophy.

Lake and Michaels would later sue Bush in attempts to recoup nearly $300,000 they said they lavished on the family in hopes of signing him as their first client.

"The general campus environment surrounding the violations troubled the committee," the NCAA infractions report said. "At least at the time of the football violations, there was relatively little effective monitoring of, among others, football locker rooms and sidelines, and there existed a general postgame locker room environment that made compliance efforts difficult."

As a preemptive move, USC self-imposed penalties for basketball, banning itself from postseason play in 2009 and '10, vacating 21 wins from the 2007–08 season that Mayo participated in, and it returned money it received through the Pac-10 for the 2008 NCAA tournament. It also lost two scholarships, was docked twenty recruiting days, and one coach was unable to recruit off-campus for the following summer. Plus, coach Tim Floyd had resigned the previous June after being accused of giving $1,000 in cash to middleman Rodney Guillory to help land Mayo.

The NCAA didn't levy any further sanctions against that program, and the same with the women's tennis team, which was cited for unauthorized phone calls made by a former player. But football was a different story entirely.

The Trojans lost thirty scholarships over three years, had to vacate 14 wins from December 2004 through the '05 season, which included one over Oklahoma in the 2004 BCS Championship Game and Bush's entire Heisman-winning season that ended with another national title game against Texas in the Rose Bowl.

"Elite athletes in high-profile sports with obvious great future earnings potential may see themselves as something apart from other student-athletes and the general student population," the NCAA report said. "Institutions need to assure that their treatment on campus does not feed into such a perception."

The NCAA also prohibited non-school personnel, outside of media and a select group of others, from practice camps and from the sidelines during games. Gone were the days of stars roaming the Coliseum. The NCAA had discussed a TV ban, but relented, saying their sanctions "adequately respond to the nature of violations and the level of institutional responsibility."

Athletic director Mike Garrett, the school's first Heisman winner, took a defiant stance when he spoke to a group of boosters at the USC Coaches' Tour at the in Burlingame, California, saying, "As I read the decision by the NCAA, all I could get out of all of this was . . . I read between the lines, and there was nothing but a lot of envy, and they wish they all were Trojans."

In a video statement, former Trojans coach Pete Carroll, who had left for the NFL's Seattle Seahawks, said he was "absolutely shocked and disappointed in the findings of the NCAA."

USC appealed the penalties and findings in 2011, asking the Infractions Appeals Committee to reduce the harshest penalties in half, arguing the bowl ban and loss of scholarships were excessive. The school pointed to NCAA decisions that were handed down after the sanctions against the Trojans, including those involving Auburn (Cam Newton was allowed to continue playing in 2010 despite the governing body ruling Newton's father had asked Mississippi State for cash during his recruitment) and Ohio State (in the scandal that cost Jim Tressel his job, five players were banned for five games in 2011 after the NCAA ruled they sold rings, jerseys, and other items and received improper benefits from a tattoo parlor).

The NCAA denied the appeal, upholding the infraction committee's findings.

"We respectfully, but vehemently, disagree with the findings of the NCAA's Infractions Appeals Committee," the university said in a statement. "Our position was that the Committee on Infractions abused its discretion and imposed penalties last June that were excessive and inconsistent with established case precedent."

Among those initial sanctions, running backs coach Todd McNair was also hit with a one-year "show-cause penalty" that kept him from recruiting. The NCAA slammed McNair for pleading ignorance of Bush's dealings. McNair, whose contract with USC wasn't renewed in 2010, filed a defamation of character suit against the NCAA in '11.

The NCAA Committee of Infractions process was at the center of the argument, which referenced emails sent between committee liaison Shep Cooper to Rondy Uphoff, a Missouri law professor who was on the 10-person committee, but was a non-voting member.

Cooper wrote on February 22, 2010, "[McNair's] a lying, morally bankrupt criminal, in my view, and a hypocrite of the highest order." In another email, Uphoff wrote to Cooper, "I fear that the committee is going to be too lenient on USC on the football violations."

The NCAA asked to have the case thrown out in 2012, but a Los Angeles Superior Court denied the request. A judge wrote that those emails "tend to show ill will or hatred."

That ruling was also appealed and in December 2015, a three-judge panel reviewed the evidence and gave the most damning take on the NCAA's investigation.

"This evidence clearly indicates that the ensuing [NCAA infractions committee] report was worded in disregard of the truth to enable the

[NCAA committee] to arrive at a predetermined conclusion that USC employee McNair was aware of the NCAA violations," said the ruling from California's Second District Court of Appeal. "To summarize, McNair established a probability that he could show actual malice by clear and convincing evidence based on the [committee's] doubts about McNair's knowledge, along with its reckless disregard for the truth about his knowledge, and by allowing itself to be influenced by nonmembers to reach a needed conclusion."

Five years after filing suit, McNair can take his case to trial. While the judges' ruling will likely add more fire to the arguments over USC's treatment and the fairness of the sanctions, it may never fix what it's done to Reggie Bush and a trophy he called "a dream come true."

****

Vince Young doesn't want it.

In September 2010—three months after the NCAA levied its sanctions—Bush announced that he was forfeiting the '05 award amid pressure after that season was vacated. In a statement released by the New Orleans Saints, for whom he was playing at the time, Bush said, "I know that the Heisman is not mine alone. Far from it. I know that my victory was made possible by the discipline and hard work of my teammates, the steady guidance of my coaches, the inspiration of the fans, and the unconditional love of my family and friends. And I know that any young man fortunate enough to win the Heisman enters into a family of sorts. Each individual carries the legacy of the award and each one is entrusted with its good name.

"It is for these reasons that I have made the difficult decision to forfeit my title as Heisman winner of 2005."

A day later, the Heisman Trust took the unprecedented step of vacating the award altogether. The season and that vote—which included a record 91.8 percent of all possible points—no longer existed.

"The Trustees of the Trust have been monitoring the NCAA investigation of Reggie Bush and USC since first announced," the Trust said in a statement. "We determined that no action was necessary by the Trust unless and until the NCAA acted and issued its report. Since the issuance of the NCAA decision vacating USC's 2005 season and declaring Reggie Bush an ineligible athlete, the Trustees have met, discussed and reviewed all information underlying this decision in an effort to exercise the due diligence and due process required of any decision regarding the awarding of the 2005 Heisman Trophy.

"As a result of Reggie Bush's decision to forfeit his title as Heisman winner of 2005, the Trustees have determined that there will be no Heisman Trophy winner for the year 2005."

But minutes before the Heisman Trust made its announcement, Texas coach Mack Brown was urging Young, his former quarterback, to say he wanted the trophy. "I told him I'd like for him to stand up and say you want it because it's important to bring it back here," Brown told the *Dallas Morning News*. "So more than anything, he's trying to help the team, he's listening to me and is trying to help the athletic department rather than himself."

But Young, who lost that vote by 933 points, took an entirely different stance when asked whether he could even accept a Heisman he didn't truly win.

"I would not want to have it, and don't want the trophy," Young told reporters. "Like I said, 2005 Reggie Bush is the Heisman Trophy winner. Why would I want it?"

That sentiment was echoed by Young's mother, Felicia, who also came to Bush's defense when she told the *Morning News*, "We're not interested in having no honor and no glory out of somebody else and trying to tear them down. They did not give Vincent the Heisman when he was there, even though I know that my son, he was the one that should have had the Heisman, but God didn't see it that way. He gave it to Reggie Bush."

But then there was the matter of *actually* giving it back.

Months before he officially took over as USC president, Max Nikias announced a number of moves in a statement, among them that Pat Haden, a former Trojans quarterback under coach John McKay, would be taking over as athletic director. He ordered the removal of any image of Bush and Mayo from any murals or displays—before students arrived back on campus in August.

He closed with this: "The university also will return Mr. Bush's 2005 Heisman Trophy to the Heisman Trophy Trust in August."

Bush said he would follow suit in September of that year, telling the *Times-Picayune* after a Saints practice, "This is definitely not an admission of guilt. For me, it's me showing my respect to the Heisman Trophy itself and to the people who have come before me and the people who'll come after me.

"I just felt like it was the best thing to do at this time. I felt like it was the most respectable thing to do, because obviously I do respect the Heisman. I do respect everything that it stands for, and respect all the people who came before me and who will come after me . . . just to silence all of the talk around it, all the negativity around it. I felt like this would be the best decision right now."

But nearly two years later, the Heisman Trust had yet to receive Bush's trophy. He had donated his copy to the San Diego Hall of Champions, which had it in storage while a number of their exhibits were being remodeled. In July 2011, the museum made the following announcement: "The San Diego Hall of Champions today returned Reggie Bush's Heisman Trophy to the Bush family. In doing so, the organization feels it is best to direct any further questions to the Bush family or the Heisman Trust."

In a 2012 appearance on *The Dan Patrick Show*, Bush said that he had personally mailed the trophy to the Trust. He is the Heisman Winner That Never Was, and while his accomplishments were wiped from history, that won't truly disappear.

"Everyone still knows Reggie Bush was the best player that year. Look at the runs. He was clearly the best player," Johnny Rodgers, the 1972 Heisman winner from Nebraska, told the AP in 2010.

"O. J. Simpson got accused of a murder and they didn't take his back. That was a far greater allegation, and they didn't find O. J. guilty on that."

> *Bush wasn't the first Heisman recipient to turn over his award, although Frank Sinkwich's move had nothing to with a scandal. Georgia's first winner, in 1942, the halfback had been keeping it in an empty bedroom in the apartment of his Bulldogs teammate, George Guisler. At the urging of Loran Smith, who would spend decades working in the school's athletic department, arrangements were made and Sinkwich gave Georgia the Heisman during halftime of a game in 1970. Because of this act, the Downtown Athletic Club would begin awarding two trophies: one for the school and one for the player.*

Bush's award now sits in a storage unit in the New York area, crammed among the memorabilia the Trust could no longer house after the Downtown Athletic Club closed its doors.

"Nobody was happy about the Reggie Bush situation," Dockery said. "I think Reggie has gone on, he's had a nice career, he's done charitable work. He [just] made some bad decisions."

****

In 1995, USC believed it had found its missing trophy. They received a call from Redondo Beach attorney Tom Loversky. As he would recount to the school, a man had come by his office and handed over what he said was O. J. Simpson's Heisman.

But as Lt. James Kenady of USC security told the *Los Angeles Times*, "It doesn't look quite right to me. I don't know what we've got."

Loversky wouldn't disclose the name of the man, nor would he say how that man had come in possession of the faux award. It was not Simpson's award, though, and the trail would go cold. That is, until Lewis Starks Jr. contacted USC to authenticate an award as the one Simpson won in 1968.

Starks didn't steal the Heisman, of that he was adamant, telling *TMZ* in September 2015 that he acquired it and a plaque of Simpson's in 1996 for a burgundy Honda Accord and $500 in cash. The man from whom he bought it—who was believed to have received it from a person involved in the theft—had the trophy buried in his backyard. Starks was in prison at the time of the award's theft, having been convicted of a separate burglary.

Shortly after he purchased the Heisman, Starks became homeless, yet he kept the trophy with him and had taken the nameplate off the award's wooden base so it could not be identified by police. He lived on street corners and storage lockers, until he called Heisman officials and later brought the items to the USC campus in 2015, asking them to authenticate the trophy.

"It's an interesting story," Los Angeles Police detective Donald Hrycyk told *The Press Enterprise* in 2015. "It illustrates taking something famous, and what are you going to do with that?"

Prosecutors would say Starks had plans of selling the Heisman in an online auction for $70,000, though as Hrycyk would later testify, "He wanted to see if he could get a finder's fee or reward."

The school notified the LAPD's Art Theft Detail and on December 16, 2014, detectives obtained a search warrant for MetroPCS records of a person they believed was connected to the missing Heisman, pointing them to Starks. After a nearly yearlong investigation, Starks was charged on September 2, 2015 in case BA439447 with one count of receiving stolen property. He was accused of, per a Los Angeles District Attorney's Office release, "being in possession of the university's copy of the trophy and the plaque, knowing that it had been stolen."

California statutes, outside of a few exceptions, limited the period in which someone could be charged with theft to three to four years. All Starks, fifty-seven, could be charged with was a felony count of receiving stolen property.

During a January 2016 hearing, an L.A. Superior Court judge denied a motion to dismiss the case or reduce it to a misdemeanor, and in July of that year, Starks—who had pleaded not guilty to a felony count in September 2015—changed his plea on the charge of receiving stolen property to no contest June 30. That same day he was sentenced to three years' formal probation.

As for the trophy and plaque, they were returned to USC. The school has not made it clear what it plans to do with the additional trophy, but its first task was having it reassembled. The award came back in three pieces—the same condition authorities discovered it in back in 2014—and an ironic state given the way Simpson, by his own doing, has seen his public image ripped apart. Regardless of the verdict in that double murder trial, he sullied the trophy in a far more detrimental way than anything that led to Bush's deletion from the award's history.

Dockery recalls the weight of that decision that faced the Heisman Trust. Eligibility is paramount, and the Trojans running back was deemed ineligible, giving the Trust little choice in the matter.

"The rules and regulations are that the winner has to be an eligible college athlete and he was declared ineligible, which made him ineligible for the trophy," Dockery said. "The trophy stands for achievement, for diligence, for hard work, for the pursuit of excellence with integrity, and the integrity is an important part [of] what we believe the Heisman stands for.

"We think it's a symbol or an icon to the youth of America—or at least the football-playing youth of America—something to strive for, something to attain, but it has to be attained correctly, by complying to the rules, and with integrity."

But then there's this: Simpson's trophy continues to be displayed in Heritage Hall, while Bush's sits in a storage unit—one standing firmly as an embarrassment, the other forced from history.

What, really, is worse for USC and for the Heisman?

CHAPTER EIGHT

THE MAKING OF A MODERN CAMPAIGN

JOHN HARRINGTON AND his son were walking up a New York City street when it first appeared in the distance, growing larger and larger as they approached, an oversized, familiar face staring back at them.

"I think the best way to describe how we both felt was just over-whelmed," the son said fifteen years later. "I remember neither one of us said very much as we got up to it."

There, across from Madison Square Garden, plastered on the side of a building, was an 80 x 100-foot billboard of Oregon quarterback Joey Harrington, or JOEY HEISMAN, as the $250,000 massive poster proclaimed.

Really, who could blame the Harringtons for being speechless in that moment as they took it in for the first time?

Father and son simply sat and looked at it, finding a spot on the wall outside of the venerable arena, neither saying very much as they continued to look up at the billboard. They sat in silence until a man in a New York University sweatshirt walked by, coming from the Harringtons' right to their left.

The local, upon seeing the duo staring at the giant poster, looked up as well as he passed and then turned his attention to the Ducks passer. He shot a look at the billboard and then again one toward the quarterback before turning a corner.

Then he stopped.

The man again peered at the giant poster and back at Harrington, then in a thick New York accent asked, "Hey, is that you?"

"Yeah, it is," Harrington replied.

"Huh," the man said. "Cool."

Then he walked away, leaving the Harringtons alone to again bask in the glow of the billboard. "Well, I guess that's a good way to put it," Joey said. "Cool."

They were taking in the idea of Ken O'Neil, a Portland businessman and Oregon alum, who was also a close friend of Nike founder and Ducks mega-booster Phil Knight. O'Neil had been in New York for the US Open tennis tournament and, while walking around the city and seeing a number of billboards, a thought struck him.

O'Neil called Oregon assistant athletic director Jim Bartko and the wheels were in motion. The school used Nike's ad agency, Wieden-Kennedy, to buy the space for the poster.

"We never get recognized by the East Coast," O'Neil told the *Register Guard* in 2001. "And to me, this is the East Coast, right here in New York. And we thought a lot of people would ask, 'What are these guys doing? Who is this guy? Where's Ore-gone?' It was kind of the ultimate tickler ad."

The price tag—which was met by eight anonymous boosters who teamed up to buy the banner—may have seemed exorbitant, but they also considered taking out a full-page ad in an issue of *Sports Illustrated* (also tossed around by the Ducks athletic department were footballs with Harrington's handprint and bobbleheads). That, on its own, would have cost about $250,000, so instead of a one-off splash, the Harrington billboard, which went up in June, was scheduled to run for three months, though it would be up for five, at no additional cost. Still, it came with its critics.

"Though the billboard seems unlikely to win Harrington the Heisman, it does serve a useful purpose," a *New York Times* editorial piece said. "It dramatizes the skewed priorities of high-powered college athletic programs. Athletic directors, awash in television revenues from football and basketball programs and generous alumni donations, are increasingly running their departments as independent fiefs. It is hard to believe there was no more constructive way for the University of Oregon to spend $250,000."

Harrington heard those concerns in Eugene, Oregon, and years later, still believes they were off base.

"There's always going to be people who said we could have used that money somewhere else," Harrington said. "Well, the reality is it wasn't like it was university funds. It was money that was donated by alums to push [football]."

That it did, helping to turn the Oregon Ducks into a national brand—and it did its part in making Harrington one of the biggest names in college football in 2001.

Of course, his play didn't hurt, either. Harrington didn't crack the top 10 in the Heisman voting in 2000 when he threw for 2,976 yards and 22 scores for the 9–2 Ducks. But coupled with a 10–1 regular season and 2,764 yards and 27 touchdowns through the air, he ended up in New York for the ceremony along with Eric Crouch of Nebraska, Miami's Ken Dorsey, and Florida's Rex Grossman.

"Had we played poorly, it would have been a giant flop," Harrington said. "But instead, we kind of woke the country up to what was going on and they started paying attention."

It didn't deliver the Heisman, though, as Crouch won, followed by Grossman, Dorsey, and Harrington. But that fourth place amounted to the highest finish in Ducks history.

"I wholeheartedly believe that I would not have been sitting in that room as a Heisman Trophy finalist without that billboard," Harrington said.

But that wasn't the end for the giant poster. In June 2003, less than a year after he had been drafted by the Detroit Lions with the No. 3 pick, Harrington returned to his alma mater and unveiled the billboard's next life. It would be cut into little bits and sold—the proceeds going to establish a scholarship fund for Oregon's Lundquist College of Business, the program through which Harrington earned his degree in business administration—each chunk of the banner mounted next to a reproduction of the "JOEY HEISMAN" banner.

"It was nice, at least, to be able to take some of that criticism and redirect it," Harrington said. "It was a nice way to kind of round the whole story out."

The billboard served its purpose, both for Harrington and the Ducks. Though in the realm of trophy marketing, the lasting impact of brash and aggressive tactics may not be its success, but its standing as the zenith of excess.

By comparison, what Budd Thalman—the father of the Heisman campaign—did in 1963 seems quaint in hindsight, but at the time, it was groundbreaking. He sent out 1,000 four-page mailers—the size of index cards—that said "Meet Roger Staubach."

"I mailed a preseason pamphlet to a lot a people," Thalman told ESPN. com in 2000. "He was on the cover and then it had his bio, some selected statistics and quotes from people around the country. People had gathered information like that before, but I don't think anyone had ever printed it."

The former Naval Academy sports information director was given clear orders: mount a campaign to put the nation on notice about Staubach, the Midshipmen's quarterback. So he sent out the cards, and once a week he'd ride a train from Annapolis to New York, statistics in hand, to attend the weekly college football writers' meetings and discuss the quarterback.

It resulted in Staubach appearing on the cover of *TIME* magazine in October, and *LIFE* was slated to follow suit the following month, with a crew shadowing the quarterback for a week for their lead story.

"Is there anything that could derail it?" Thalman asked a *LIFE* magazine spokesperson.

"Only some kind of catastrophe," they replied.

One week before the issue was to hit newsstands, the nation was faced with a catastrophe, as John F. Kennedy was assassinated. *LIFE* instead ran a thirty-six-page special issue, and Staubach's cover was scrapped.

The country had more important concerns at the time, but the voters had, indeed, met Roger Staubach. He ran away with the Heisman, winning by 1,356 points over Georgia Tech quarterback Billy Lothridge.

"Someone called me 'the Father of Heisman Hype,' and I've been trying to live it down ever since," Thalman told ESPN.com.

To be fair, a year before Staubach's win, Oregon State SID John Eggers would copy quarterback Terry Baker's statistics from every game on a mimeograph machine and send them out to voters. With postage at five cents, it's doubtful that Eggers spent more than $100.

"For the eastern writers who never had seen Oregon State—and games were not on TV then like they are now—they would have known very little about what was going out here, but for what information he spoon-fed to them," Baker told Oregon State in a 2014 Q&A. "So that was very creative at that time."

Schools would soon up the ante. In 1967, UCLA sent out 1,000 color brochures calling quarterback Gary Beban "The Great One," as he went on to win, and Notre Dame went so far as changing the pronunciation of a candidate's name.

As the story goes, someone said, "There's Joe Theismann" (saying it as *Theesman*), and Notre Dame's SID, Roger Valdiserri, replied, "No, it's Theismann, as in Heisman."

South Bend Tribune sports editor Joe Doyle would credit Valdiserri in his column, then a year later, *Sports Illustrated* used "rhymes with Heisman" in its December 9, 1968 issue.

In his 1987 autobiography *Theismann*, the QB recalled Valdiserri calling him into his office.

"There's the Heisman Trophy, Joe, and I think we should pronounce your name as *Thighsman*," the SID told him.

Theismann called his father, who would tell him that despite their saying "Theesman," his grandmother insisted it was "Thighsman." The family had registered in American schools as *Theismann* after they had emigrated from Austria, because it was the easiest way people could read the name.

"Well, my grandmother pronounces it that way," Theismann would tell him. "What the heck, let's do it."

The Heisman may have been in his name, but it wasn't in his future, as Stanford's Jim Plunkett beat him out during his senior season of 1970. Theismann earned 242 first-place votes to Plunkett's 510 first-place votes, coming in 819 points behind.

No Heisman campaign would be quite that permanent—family history not withstanding—but by the 1980s, the outlandish and gimmicky was becoming more commonplace.

In 1980, Pitt mailed out life-sized posters of 6-foot-2, 225-pound defensive end Hugh Green, and four years later, Clemson would repeat the process in promoting 6-foot-3, 335-pound nose guard William "The Refrigerator" Perry (the Tigers gave a nod to that effort in 2009 with another poster, this one for running back C. J. Spiller).

BYU sprinkled rolled oats into envelopes along with information about center Bart Oates in '81, and that same year, Richmond pushed running back Barry Redden, including T-shirts, hats, and calendars promoting him for the award to go along with its weekly reports. Georgia campaigned for Herschel Walker in '82 by mailing out weekly updates on its running back in mailers that included "Herschel for Heisman" artwork.

West Virginia got creative in '83 for Jeff Hostetler, celebrating the quarterback with 45-rpm records of a ballad titled "Ole Hoss," which was put to the tune of the theme from the television show *Bonanza* and sung by country artists Mark Newhouse and Brad Reeves. "It's really bad," Hostetler said in 1983. "It sure isn't a top 40 hit."

Temple followed suit by creating a sixteen-page comic book about running back Paul Palmer in 1986, but the Owls' push also included a celebrity cameo. When golf legend Arnold Palmer—a Latrobe, Pennsylvania, native—was playing in a tournament near campus, university officials took Paul to the course for a photo of the two. They mailed it out to voters with the caption: "Pennsylvania Has Two Palmers."

Winners Andre Ware of Houston (1989) and BYU's Ty Detmer ('90), had their own campaigns, with Houston making up for a lack of television exposure due to NCAA sanctions by sending out a weekly flier to potential voters for "Air" Ware that looked like an airline time-table; BYU mailed out cardboard ties for Detmer that opened to reveal the passer's stats.

Washington State greeted voters with an envelope containing a single leaf for quarterback Ryan Leaf in 1997, and then five years later the school delivered a truly tongue-in-cheek promotion for another quarterback, Jason Gesser.

In retaliation of Oregon's six-figure banner for Harrington, the Cougars put up a 25-by-15-foot poster of Gesser on the side of a 10-story grain elevator in Dusty, Washington, on the road that ran from Pullman to Seattle. The cost? A mere $2,500, or 1/100th of what it took for the Ducks to have Joey Heisman's likeness outside MSG.

"Jason and I still laugh about that," Harrington said.

This was largely the playground of non-traditional powers or programs promoting non-traditional candidates, especially entering the 2000s. Sure, Ohio State would make a play for offensive lineman Orlando Pace in 1996, distributing magnets that brought the pancake block to the forefront, showing a stack of flapjacks with butter melting down the side. The reality is, during this era, the Michigans, Notre Dames, and USCs of the college football world didn't need to do much to get the word out on their players.

Said Trojans SID Tim Tessalone to the *Honolulu Advertiser* in 2005, a year after Matt Leinart claimed his trophy and before Reggie Bush would go on to win, "they are going to get plenty of attention, anyway."

But the schools that didn't already have a fraternity within the fraternity of Heisman winners could be aided by the publicity. Hence, Marshall making Byron Leftwich bobbleheads in '02; Memphis's die-cast cars for running back DeAngelo Williams in '05, which ran about $8 per car (the school shrewdly recouped that expense, selling another 1,500 cars for $30 apiece); Missouri's Chase Daniel View-Master-style slide players that included a slide of Daniel's highlights (those came at a cost of $25,000 for 2,500 of them); Boise State sending out "Ian for Heisman" DVDs in '06 for running back Ian Johnson (a tactic Hawaii also did in '07 with "A Colt Following" in hyping quarterback Colt Brennan), and Rutgers's Ray Rice binoculars in '07 that invited voters to "See Ray Run."

This was the world in which Oregon's anonymous boosters forked over a quarter of a million dollars to supply the football program and its star quarterback with prime real estate in the media capital of the world. Even if it didn't bring the Ducks their first Heisman (something that, ironically, quarterback Marcus Mariota would do in 2014 with little to no push whatsoever), it aided the program in reaching the country's upper echelon.

"I honestly think—and I'm not just saying this because it was something personal, and because of the actual physical side of it—it was one of the biggest and best marketing campaigns, definitely in Heisman history, but maybe in college football [history]," Harrington said in 2015.

That is, until Baylor went and completely changed the game ten years after Oregon's billboard.

****

Heath Nielsen and the rest of Baylor's football sports information department convened in the summer of 2011 eyeing a goal that—from a purely historical standpoint—seemed as likely as a blizzard hitting the Waco, Texas campus.

"Let's get him to New York," Nielsen said about Robert Griffin III, the Bears' junior quarterback. "If everything falls our way, hopefully he can get invited as a finalist."

To be fair, their task may have been even more far-fetched than a colossal snowfall. An average of 1.2 inches had fallen on the Central Texas city in the last thirty years and in the previous seventy-six Heisman votes, the school produced just two players who were in the top 10, QBs Larry Isbell (who was seventh in 1951) and Don Trull (fourth in '63). Neither was really a factor, with Isbell taking twenty first-place nods, in coming in 1,614 points behind Princeton's Dick Kazmaier, and Trull received twenty-nine firsts as he trailed Staubach by 1,607 points.

But on December 31, 1946, Waco had been bombarded with twenty inches of snow. So if Mother Nature could find her way to bring the unexpected to the Heart of Texas, well, Nielsen and Co. had a chance to do the same.

"We were just young and naive enough to try pretty much anything, and to just kind of be creative and go for silly stuff," Nielsen said.

The preseason perceptions were an uphill battle. Griffin was eleventh in oddsmaker Bodog's initial betting line, trailing Stanford's Andrew Luck (9/2), Oklahoma's Landry Jones (13/2), South Carolina's Marcus Lattimore (7/1), Michigan's Denard Robinson (15/2), Oregon's LaMichael James (15/2), Alabama's Trent Richardson (12/1), Oklahoma State's Justin Blackmon (15/1), Boise State's Kellen Moore (15/1), Arkansas's Knile Davis (15/1), and Oklahoma's Ryan Broyles (15/1). That put him fifth in the Southwest voting region and fourth among Big 12 players.

There was also an internal factor playing against Griffin. His coach, Art Briles, was initially reluctant, especially with the fact that his quarterback was only a junior. "I had to get coach's green light before the season," Nielsen said. "He is old-school enough that he's not big into 'Let's highlight an individual and if you have to, let's make it a senior.'"

But Briles—whose tenure in Waco would come to an end amid a sexual assault scandal in May 2016—relented, understanding the value a campaign had—much like Oregon with Harrington—in utilizing Griffin as a launching pad for Baylor. It was, after all, coming off a 7–6 season under its fourth-year coach, which amounted to its first winning record in fifteen years, and had capped it by being hammered by Illinois in the Texas Bowl 38–14.

"We didn't have the success on the field, we didn't have the television presence. We were going to do everything in our power—and not necessarily fan-wise—but to get that name to influential, key media," Nielsen said. "The folks who were actually doing the talking and the sharing [of] the Heisman names. We wanted them to hear about our quarterback."

But how? In order to overcome stigmas, Baylor's staff knew it couldn't follow normal campaign templates and be successful; the approach was going to have to be unique. So during those summer meetings, the rule was "Don't laugh at any idea. Let's put it all on a piece of paper."

They began the push at Big 12 media days with a run-of-the-mill play: handing out a reporter's notepad. It featured a photo of Griffin with his hands held high to signal a touchdown, and included branding of an RG3 shield and was littered with quotes from writers calling the passer the "fastest man to ever play quarterback in college football," "like a magician," "as exciting as there is in college football," and "breathtaking," to pick a few.

The reaction? There were some snickers.

"Baylor quarterback Robert Griffin is not going to win the Heisman," a *Star-Telegram* writer proclaimed.

The school, though, was just getting started.

"My earliest thoughts were, 'We've got to be somewhere in the digital/social realm, because that's where the eyeballs are now,'" Nielsen said. "It's funny sitting here in 2016, thinking back that doing a Facebook page and having a Twitter account was cutting edge, but it kind of was back then."

The night of the Bears' season opener against No. 14 TCU—which was coming off a Rose Bowl victory over Wisconsin—the school took the first step into that realm with a website promoting Griffin, BU-RG3.com. The quarterback responded by throwing a career-best 5 touchdown passes on 21 of 27 passing for 359 yards, ran for 38 yards on 10 carries, and even had a reception for 15 yards in a 50–48 victory.

"After we beat TCU, that's when we kind of looked at our list and said 'OK. We're going for this,'" Nielsen said.

Along with making Griffin available to any writer—nationally or regionally—who wanted to talk to him, they created "RG3 for Heisman" Facebook and Twitter pages and did weekly YouTube videos entitled *30 with the THIIIRD*, in which teammates would ask Griffin questions in rapid-fire fashion. Baylor used Facebook to allow fans to enter to win a prize package by sharing photos on their Facebook walls, but where the school truly set off a phenomenon on the platform was after Griffin passed for a program-best 479 yards and 4 touchdowns, including a 34-yarder to Terrance Williams with eight seconds remaining, to knock off No. 5 Oklahoma 45–38 on November 19.

A 59–24 loss to third-ranked Oklahoma State on October 29 dropped the Bears to 4–3, and Nielsen remembers people asking how much longer they planned on pushing Griffin with the wheels seemingly coming off Baylor's season. "Which is a little awkward, because, let's say your candidate isn't going to do so well, how do you bow out when you dove in full-force?" Nielsen said.

But as Griffin's star rose in national consciousness after that performance against the Sooners, it proved to be perfect timing and Baylor asked fans to "Join the Third," which entailed attaching "III" to their names.

"That's when it went from, a kind of what the institution is putting out there and aiming it at the media, and that's when the grassroots, groundswell fan movement started," Nielsen said.

Thousands of fans obliged, and five years later, it's a movement that remains one of the more impactful tactics that Baylor employed.

"That really, really took off," Nielsen said. "To this day, I can list out twenty things we did, and that's the one thing that people remember. It's just the ingenious, new thing, and it's funny, because to this day there are still some Baylor fans that still have the III on their Facebook page. They never reverted to their real name."

It was, in essence, brand building on a level few had ever accomplished in the nascent days of social media. Fans were engaged and voters educated, but Nielsen had a nostalgic streak that he wanted fed.

With nineteen years in the sports information game, he remembered the splash BYU made with its Detmer ties, and what Washington State accomplished by mailing out leafs. He wanted to capture that bit of Heisman campaigns past by giving media members something tangible as well.

A local businessman had caught wind that Baylor's staff was looking to create something and approached Nielsen with an idea that fit that bill. He brought in a prototype of a Wheaties box that said "Heisman" across the top in place of the cereal's name and featured an action shot of the quarterback. Where a normal cereal box would include a rundown of its ingredients, it had football references.

Nielsen opened the box and inside was cereal, along with a prize—a small video screen that could be loaded with highlights of Griffin.

"I was like 'Wow,'" Nielsen said. "He was really selling me on it."

The SID already had one idea in mind from their summer brainstorming session, a series of football cards, which in taking into account printing costs, shipping, and supplies, was estimated to run $10,000. With the school working off a list of upward of 700 voters they had identified, the entire run of cards would work out to 12 to 18 cents each. As he took in the box and the working MP4 player he asked the man,

"How much would this cost?"

"Oh," he replied, "it wouldn't be that much. I think we could be able to produce these for about $60 each."

"I'm not a math whiz, but my brain took a couple of seconds trying to multiply … and I'm trying to do the math of how much this would cost, and it was just crazy," Nielsen said.

The idea wasn't to send out the cereal boxes to hundreds of voters, just a few high-profile figures to get exposure on ESPN's *College GameDay*

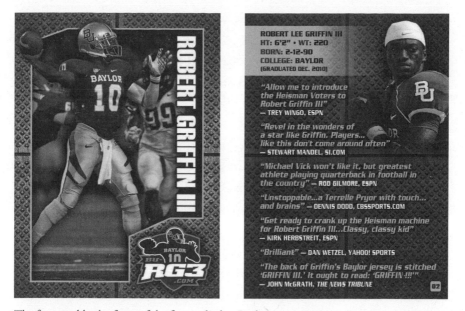

The front and back of one of the five cards that Baylor sent to Heisman voters to promote Robert Griffin III in 2011.
(Baylor Athletic Department)

or in the pages of *Sports Illustrated*—but it wasn't that approach that Nielsen was looking for in trying to push a player at a program that had been a perennial doormat.

"I was taking the other approach," he said. "I wanted to hit everybody with something small rather than a big, expensive piece."

Northwestern, another oft-overlooked school, had gone that route, putting the spotlight on quarterback Dan Persa by mailing out purple shoe-sized boxes that included two purple, seven-pound weights—he wore No. 7—that said "Persa Strong." They arrived at the doorsteps of about seventy writers with an accompanying release that said "Persa Strong highlights Persa as the complete student-athlete. Strong on the field, in the classroom and in the community."

Baylor would create five RG3 cards, mailed in plastic cases, with each having a different focus. The first, which was sent out days before the season opener against the Horned Frogs, was approached as a teaser of sorts, with one side featuring a close-up of the back of Griffin's jersey and the RG3 logo. The other side said, "In the 2011 Heisman race, keep your eye on the third ..."

One that included quotes from media members followed, and another was centered on Griffin's success off the field, showing him receiving his undergraduate degree (in political science) in December 2010, and listed his academic awards. There was also a card that showcased Griffin the teammate, highlighting his offensive line and included the quote, "If I win an individual award, it's based on what I've done with the guys around me. Without those guys, I'm nothing." The final card was an action shot with the hashtag #JOINTHETHIRD.

The use of digital assets earned Nielsen and Co. acclaim, and while the football cards were another means of reaching those who maybe hadn't embraced social media to that point, they ended up resonating more than Baylor's SID could have expected.

"I will say, when it was all said and done, the part that surprised me the most, and I think the part that made the most impact was those physical football cards," Nielsen said. "All it would take, you send them one in the mail, and they do their advertising for you, because they put it on their social account and then you're getting exponential number of eyeballs seeing it, and just because you sent them a football card. . . . I actually think that old-school piece of it was really, really key."

As was Griffin's play. In throwing for 3,998 yards and 36 touchdowns to 6 interceptions, along with 644 rushing yards and 9 more scores, he was the nation's only player with at least 3,000 yards passing and 300 rushing. His career numbers of 10,000 yards through the air and 2,000 on the ground made him the third player in FBS history to hit those numbers and the first from a major conference.

Griffin would win by 280 points over the preseason favorite Luck, garnering 405 first-place votes to 247 for the Cardinal quarterback. He also did it on a 9–3 team, tying Tim Tebow ('07) and Ricky Williams ('98) for the fewest victories by a winner since Tim Brown won at 8–4 Notre Dame in 1987.

"This is unbelievably believable," Griffin said in his speech. "It's unbelievable because in the moment, we're all amazed when great things happen. But it's believable because great things don't happen without hard work."

Griffin's campaign was about fully embracing the right space at the right time. That same year, Stanford launched a microsite for Luck and also had a seven-minute presentation by coach David Shaw stumping for his quarterback, Oklahoma State had Twitter and Facebook pages for quarterback Brandon Weeden and Blackmon called "Weeden-2Blackmon," and Wisconsin had one for quarterback Russell Wilson (the Badgers would get a finalist that year, though it wasn't Wilson, but rather running back Montee Ball).

"It wasn't like we were breaking new ground, even though we get credit for stuff like that. I think we got a little bit fortunate timing-wise that that's the way the world was turning," Nielsen said. "We were on the front edge of that and were willing to push it hard. We did the Twitter, we did the Facebook, we did the full-blown website, a lot of the video portion of things."

They also, more importantly, in helping to elevate the effectiveness of how they pushed Griffin, helped Baylor win.

That resulted in a 10 percent rise in donations to the Bear Foundation, the school's licensing royalties rose more than 50 percent, and it saw increases in ticket sales, sponsorship deals, and its regional television contract. Per media measurement group General Sentiment, Baylor earned what amounted to $14 million in media coverage surrounding the campaign.

Baylor may not have reinvented Heisman hype, but it leveraged digital assets and the physical to set the stage for a new kind of campaign.

"[Griffin] winning that award on that evening in New York was the biggest athletic moment in Baylor sports history," Nielsen said. "I don't know that many would argue that it didn't put Baylor on the map."

These days, the brunt of campaigns are waged in digital fashion. Stanford launched WildCaff.com in 2015 for Christian McCaffrey, which included an ingenious 360-degree video experience of the running back on the field, and Oklahoma had a dancing, eight-bit version of quarterback Baker Mayfield in GIF form and used it with the hashtag #ShakeNBake. The old-school approach still has its place though, with Kansas State focusing on finalist-to-be Collin Klein's toughness with a mailer that had an oversized Band-Aid; Northern Illinois promoted Jordan Lynch—who made it to New York in '13—with a lunch box; Nebraska created Ameer Abdullah AA batteries (or more specifically, AA8s, to highlight the running back's number) in '14, with a package that included a warning label that said the Cornhusker "can cause shock to opposing defenses" and "prolonged exposure could cause an explosion on the national scene"; and in '15, Colorado State sent out 500 packages of microwave popcorn to hype up wide receiver Rashard "Hollywood" Higgins.

"I think that is still super effective," Nielsen said. "If everyone is going digital now, that might do a little bit more to make you stand out because of their rarity."

If Joey Harrington represents the extremes of Heisman campaigning, Griffin is the antithesis, fueled by a largely viral push with a price tag of less than a tenth of Oregon's in 2001.

Their paths would cross in 2014, when Griffin—on an off-day from the Washington Redskins—was back in Waco for the opening of McLane Stadium and the unveiling of his statue. Harrington, meanwhile, was part of FOX Sports 1's broadcast team for the game.

Griffin was walking through the press box when Nielsen stopped him and took him over to meet Harrington and the rest of the TV team as they were eating and compiling pregame notes.

The two quarterbacks struck up a conversation when Harrington told him, "You went all the way and got the award I was trying for."

"Yeah," a nearby Nielsen chimed in, laughing. "I think he had a better SID than you did."

CHAPTER NINE
THE PHOTOGRAPHER WHO LINKS PAST AND FUTURE

NEARLY ALONE, BUT for their anxieties and each other, as they waited out the final minutes in the green room before the airing of the 2009 Heisman Trophy ceremony was set to begin, Mark Ingram turned to Tim Tebow for help.

The Florida quarterback was an old hand when it came to the setting. Having won the award in 2007, Tebow stood as the only three-time finalist in history, giving him a calm in these proceedings that Ingram sorely needed to tap into.

"Tim," the Alabama running back, and that year's trophy recipient, said, "I'm nervous."

"Let's go over in the corner and pray," Tebow replied.

The two did, bowing their heads together, and Kelly Kline knew it was an opportunity she let pass her by.

"I think there was sometimes when I was nervous at the beginning and sometimes I didn't photograph some moments," said Kline, the Heisman Trust's photographer and the only outsider privy to those minutes before the show begins.

"Like I didn't photograph Mark Ingram and Tim Tebow praying in the corner. I kind of wish I had, but then again the photo might not have told what was happening. It might have been just two guys with their noses in the corner, so you really wouldn't have known what it

Heisman Trust photographer Kelly Kline with Alabama running
back Mark Ingram, the 2009 winner.
(Emilee Ramsier / Photo from Kelly Kline/Heisman Trust)

was, but it was still an interesting story. . . . but now it's just a story. I
don't have an image to support it."

Two years later when winner Baylor's Robert Griffin III, Wisconsin's Montee Ball, Stanford's Andrew Luck, LSU's Tyrann Mathieu,
and Alabama's Trent Richardson joined hands in a circle to pray, Kline
didn't hesitate.

"You get over that as a photographer," she said. "I think at first I was
nervous, 'Oh, they're having a moment. I don't want to photograph it,'
and I think that was just me being a rookie photographer. You learn
after you take enough photos that after awhile it's not about you anymore. You just capture it . . . I don't worry about ruining the moment."

As the Trust's official photographer she is the proverbial fly on the
wall during the Heisman weekend—which stretches from the players'
arrival in New York on Friday through the Monday night gala event—
standing as the visual chronicler of the award and the lens through

which Griffin, Ingram, and Tebow take their place alongside Davey O'Brien, John David Crow, and Steve Spurrier.

Throughout that four-day run of schedule Kline takes hundreds of images, and has multiple hard drives housing more than a decade's worth of ceremonies. There are candid moments of the players sharing New York City together, among them a 2008 shot of Texas's Colt McCoy giving the Longhorns hand gesture and Oklahoma's Sam Bradford countering it by pointing the horns down in his own rendition; and Tebow and then-Florida coach Urban Meyer walking through Times Square moments after the quarterback's 2007 victory.

"It's real, raw emotions," Kline, an Atlanta resident, said.

Kline also attends the Sunday night dinner at Battery Gardens. An opportunity for the newest and past winners to unwind, it's attended by roughly 125 people. At that small, intimate affair, Kline has been privy to the likes of Billy Sims and Archie Griffin dancing with Cam Newton, but the value of that event is tied to its private nature, hence those photos rarely, if ever, are seen by the public.

But it's in the green room where Kline has seen emotion expressed in so many very different ways. While Ingram, Tebow, and the finalists that joined Griffin leaned on faith, Auburn's Newton instead set the tone with his charisma. Before the 2010 presentation, he sat on a couch with Luck, Oregon's LaMichael James, and Boise State's Kellen Moore and Kline took a photo of the four all together, simply smiling.

"Why they were all on that one, tiny couch, I have no idea," Kline said. "But they were all there together, crammed up tight with nervous energy. They were all smiling, but it all started with Cam. Cam's personality really just took over and his smile made everyone else smile."

In 2015, Alabama's Derrick Henry, Stanford's Christian McCaffrey, and Clemson's Deshaun Watson took the opposite approach, each sitting by themselves and barely talking to one another.

"The last few moments before the show goes on, I find, are very fascinating," Kline said. "They clear the room. It's like five minutes before the show goes live. Guys always act differently at that time."

That's a side of the proceedings that few will ever experience, though those images are rarely seen by those not associated with the winner or the Heisman Trust. Among all those photos Kline creates, it's two annually that will stand the test of time: one you can't escape and the one you never knew existed.

The one you know comes seconds after the winner gets the trophy, that photo that appears on countless websites and in newspapers across the country. It is *the* Heisman photo, the reason that Kline is in attendance during the ceremony.

It comes with its own set of challenges, the biggest being that there is no do-over, no directing the action. The biggest variable is the unknown.

"It's a very unique situation that I'm the only photographer in the room. There's not another job that I have where that happens. I shoot a lot of other sporting events, and there's always a lot of photographers. There's a lot of pressure to get the shot, because I do recognize I'm pretty much the only one—but I just take more frames. I take as much as I can."

Winners have raised the award—in 2013, Florida State's Jameis Winston hoisted it above his head—and others have, upon realizing it weighs 25 pounds, dropped it down, which creates havoc for keeping the camera focused. Texas A&M's Johnny Manziel made life easy as he literally stood on stage posing with his Heisman in '12, and then there was Henry, who leaned down and kissed his trophy in '15.

"Some years you just do it better than others," Kline said. "It really depends on the guy too. Does he lift it for two seconds or six seconds? You can't capture more than what happens. Johnny Manziel held the thing up for 15 seconds … you can get 200 frames in 15 seconds. Derrick Henry just went straight for the kiss. He never held it, he just went down and kissed it. So that was a little tricky.

"So what the guy does with the trophy really depends on how iconic that photo is."

She has yet to miss that moment—"Knock on wood," she said—but she did come close during Ingram's win, "and that kind of put the fear of God into me." She began having her assistant Emilee Ramsier in the back of the room covering a second angle, a luxury that paid off when Winston raised the award and Ramsier had a better image.

"You just don't know what the guy is going to do and it's scary sometimes," Kline said. "I always mentally prepare for it. You're just ready for it."

In a period in time in which everyone has a camera in their pocket, and the ability to instantly deliver it via social media platforms, there's an undeniable quaintness about Kline's situation and responsibility, none of which is lost on her.

"I do recognize the importance of it. . . . When you see these photos from years and years ago, they are so cool looking," Kline said. "So I recognize the body of work now that I'm taking will someday be that history. It literally is the history."

The body of work Kline references spans a decade, dating back to the 2005 ceremony in which Reggie Bush beat Texas's Vince Young and his USC teammate Matt Leinart. Kline was one year removed from graduating from the Hallmark Institute of Technology, a career turn for the former weekend sports anchor for Augusta, Georgia's Channel 12, and she was hired by events company Brightroom to shoot what it described to her as "a high school football banquet, but for grownups."

"They really didn't understand the prestige and honor behind the Heisman," Kline said.

The company, which specialized in corporate events, only offered a basic approach, and Kline saw a bigger opportunity to supply the Heisman with a greater breadth of imagery. When Brightroom called back in 2006 to book Kline again, she decided to call the Heisman Trust with an idea. She pitched them on the plan that she could cut out the middleman and give the Trust more content with an archive that she and the trophy's keepers would co-own.

"Looking back now, it was a little bit of a ballsy move, but that's what you have to do as a business owner, I guess," Kline said. "For me I just saw opportunities where I could supply more creative services that a big corporate company that was just cut-and-dry how they did things really wouldn't meet the needs of the Heisman."

They bit, and from Ohio State's Troy Smith's win in 2006 on, Kline has photographed the festivities as the Trust's business partner, with one bit of instruction—*try not to disrupt television*, they would tell her "because the show is really about TV," Kline said.

And it's in aiding that aspect of the trophy—the TV product—where Kline has helped to continue a visual Heisman staple.

Manziel returned as a finalist the year after his victory, and during the walkthrough the day of the ceremony, he saw his portrait for the first time hanging among the legendary names that came before him. In a very meta move, the quarterback took a selfie with it. Two years later, Henry used a similar moment during the rehearsal to take his photo with the image of a fellow Crimson Tide running back.

"He was enamored by the portrait of Mark Ingram," Kline said.

Watch any of ESPN's ceremonies and, stretched across the background behind the podium will be those portraits of the past winners. Once hanging in the Downtown Athletic Club's trophy room, the first 60-plus were the work of former Oklahoma All-American wide receiver Tommy McDonald, who finished third in the 1956 voting when Notre Dame's Paul Hornung won.

Technically, they weren't created by his hands, but rather by the hands of one of the team of artists that he employed at Tommy McDonald Enterprises, though the ex-Sooner's signature does appear on the bottom of the paintings. His company had stretched from the first winner, Jay Berwanger (1935), through Wisconsin's Ron Dayne (1999).

McDonald had lucked his way into the business. When he was with the Philadelphia Eagles, he had autographed a photo for a fan, and after a game, that fan greeted him with a 16 x 20 painting.

"It was fantastic," McDonald told ESPN.com in 2003. "He tells me that he wants me to have it because he's a big fan of mine and he appreciated me sending him out an autographed picture. I wanted to pay him for it, but he wouldn't let me."

McDonald gave the artist a photo of his wife, who had an upcoming birthday, and asked for another panting. Then it hit him: "I thought about it and of all the rings, watches, trophies and silver trays, nobody gives something like [the portraits]," he said. "I'm telling you it was a gold mine. Hey, what guy is going to throw rocks at his own portrait? Nobody is going to hate himself. It just blossomed into a great business."

But when he retired, the Trust was missing that ability to link the winners. With the help of ESPN, they had found a shortcut and started manipulating photos to make them look like those portraits. Beginning with Florida State's Chris Weinke in 2000 they were working with photos from the schools that had been taken during preseason shoots—and there was a drop in quality that was all too noticeable to Kline.

"A school headshot is very different than this Heisman hero portrait or how they'd always been in the artists' renderings," she said.

The photographer would suggest that to properly link the trophy's past to its future, they should pay homage to those McDonald paintings by replicating the poses and taking advantage of modern technology.

"I think more than anything I felt like there was a need for it," she said. "I was like, 'We can take this to another level and make it work a little better with the past and make the present feel like they all work together.'"

Beginning with Tebow in '07, she has held a 10-minute portrait session with each winner on the Monday after the ceremony. She'll take note of the old renderings, shoulder angles, and the different perspectives—with one caveat. A number of the old images showed the winner looking off into the distance, a trend she opted not to continue.

"I don't really shoot that way," she said. "I've shot a few off-camera and none of them have been edited into the process, but I don't do the final edit. But I do think of camera angle—whether I'm above a guy or below a guy, if he's turned a little bit.

"I go through a whole series of 'he turns left, he turns right; I go high, I go low.' I might get 10–15 different angles and when you go through that process, some of them stand out and look better than others."

From Kline's images, Rob Whalen, the executive director of the Heisman Trophy Trust, will send a select few to Dan Cunningham, ESPN's creative director. Charged with building the environment for the ceremony, Cunningham decides which photo will become the rendering we eventually see. ESPN senior artists then add effects to the image before cutting out the headshot and placing it on a painted background.

"I look at the face . . . the smile means a lot," Cunningham said in 2013 of the selection process. "I want to make sure it's *the* shot. It's representative of what he'll do for the rest of his life."

That's the message Kline works to convey during the photo session.

"There's not any huge rocket science that goes into the execution of the picture, but it's understanding the subject and getting them into that frame of mind of 'This is going to be your Heisman portrait that's going to go up on the wall forever. How do you want to look?'"

Henry, so enthralled by Ingram's image, took it seriously. He asked to see every shot and pushed for more photos of him straight on with a slight turn. "It was just his personality . . . and he didn't want to smile," Kline said. "Some guys don't want to smile. Cam Newton wanted to smile. RG3 wanted to smile. Derrick? No. No smiles. Their own personality plays into it a little bit."

That's what allowed Kline to take an admitted risk with Griffin. When the Baylor quarterback won and flashed his Superman socks, Kline was hit with inspiration. She asked her assistant to purchase a costume and a pair of $10 black-rimmed sunglasses with the lenses removed.

"I asked [Griffin] first, 'What do you think of this idea? Because we've only got about 10 minutes to do it,'" Kline said. "He said, 'I love it. I love it. Let's do it.'"

The result was Clark Kent in transformation, the Heisman winner with his trophy in front of him as he wore the glasses frames with his open dress shirt revealing the Man of Steel's logo underneath. Griffin kept those frames, wearing them to the Monday night banquet—a white-tie affair. They stayed on during a speech the Bears star made to the crowd, and he continued wearing them until coach Art Briles took them off so he could sport them himself when he addressed the attendees.

That Superman shot, of course, wasn't the image that appeared as Griffin's portrait. In that, he's smiling while wearing his No. 10 Baylor jersey, his shot nearly indistinguishable in style and execution from that of Andre Ware, the 1989 winner from Houston.

While that painting, and so many before and after it, were crafted by McDonald's artists, they are more closely related to Kline's photos than you'd think—because what you see during the ceremony is actually Kline's work.

When the Sports Museum of America opened in May 2008 in Lower Manhattan, it was to serve as the official home of the Heisman Trophy after the Downtown Athletic Club closed its doors in the aftermath of the September 11 terrorist attacks. That included housing the original trophy and creating an exhibit using Heisman artifacts and memorabilia, including the oil paintings.

Not the actual paintings, though. They remained in storage, and Kline had been commissioned by the museum to photograph each of them for its collage. But while the Sports Museum of America was closed by February 2009—it cited low attendance and $6 million in cost overruns—those copies of the Heisman winner's portraits had another life as part of ESPN's set. So in reality, the paintings that line the back wall during the announcement are actually photographs Kline took of the originals.

It's a contribution to the Heisman that, despite millions seeing every year, is hidden in plain sight.

"I don't want it to be about the photographer," she said. "It needs to be about that moment in time."

Still, that front-row seat for history has provided a rather unique perspective.

During a visit to Twitter's headquarters on West 17th Street during his victory lap of media appearances, Henry was greeted with a large screen showing one of his tweets from 2012. "I'm gone win Heisman #Goals #DreamingBig!" he wrote. That boast, he would disclose, came on the heels of his posing with Manziel and his trophy while the Yulee, Florida, product was in NYC as a finalist for the U.S. Army Player of the Year.

When Kline went back through her archives from Manziel's three-year-old photo shoot, there was the photographic evidence: the Texas A&M quarterback in a tuxedo posing with his trophy; next to him is Henry in his Army All-American jersey.

Kline's job, as she puts it, is "to chronicle the Heisman, and I feel very strongly about that. This is historic."

And, every once in a while, prophetic.

EPILOGUE

An Impact Beyond the Game

IN HIS EARLY dealings with the keepers of the Heisman Trophy, 2001 winner Eric Crouch was struck by a surreal and ominous thought.

"I was more concerned, being in those meetings, if the Heisman was going to be around," the Nebraska quarterback said.

The aftermath of the September 11 terrorist attacks would, like nothing before it, test the foundation of the American institution, but in the years before the Heisman had already proven it was, if nothing else, resilient.

In 1960, when the DAC boasted a membership of 4,500 and had more on a waiting list, the athletic and social club to the elite included a fitness center, a 137-room hotel, seven banquet rooms, and an Olympic-sized swimming pool among its amenities. By 1998, that number of members was under 1,300. Its lower Manhattan home was in need of repairs and the club had filed for Chapter 11 bankruptcy in 1998 and owed New York City $5 million in back taxes.

A Federal Bankruptcy Court judge was considering ordering the club to be sold—likely to investors Richard Born and Steven Caspi, who had purchased the DAC's $8.3 million mortgage. They offered to lease the club the space it needed, but the sides were at odds. The duo required the Heisman be displayed in the building's lobby year-round, to which DAC president William J. Dockery replied, "We don't want the trophy to be sullied by the likes of these real estate speculators."

A sale would have potentially meant the end of the club, and, in turn, the Heisman.

The DAC dodged the sale in what Dockery called "the legal equivalent of a late touchdown pass." A shot in the arm would come in the form of a three-year, $1.5 million corporate sponsorship with American Suzuki in the summer of 1999, and a year later, more relief came in the form of Connecticut real estate investment firm Cheslock, Bakker & Associates.

It made a $9.85 million payment to the DAC's mortgage holder, effectively ending the DAC's 14-month bankruptcy battle. The firm had also agreed to buy the upper twenty-two floors of the thirty-five-story building at 19 West Street for $8 million and provided upward of $11.5 million to satisfy the club's remaining creditors. As part of the deal, Cheslock Bakker would sell thirteen floors back to the Downtown Athletic Club for $8 million, meaning the club could keep its cherished location, and the award with which it was synonymous.

The DAC had turned the corner, and did so with the assistance of the Heisman Trust, a nine-member committee that in October 1999 filed paperwork to become the holders of the Heisman Trophy trademark. Its mission, as its filing said, is "promoting interest, excellence and sportsmanship in intercollegiate football through the medium of an annual award."

But it was also a maneuver to protect that asset regardless of what happened to the DAC. Even if someone acquired the club, it wouldn't take ownership of the Heisman as well, but for these purposes, the Trust was the guardians of the trophy and it delegated the administration to the DAC.

Both the award and its home had been saved; then 9/11 came and altered that reality.

When the World Trade Center towers collapsed, the upper levels of the club were being gutted and the windows on the 14th floor and up were opened for added ventilation. Dust and debris from the attacks filled the rooms and overwhelmed the air ducts. While there was no structural damage, the building would need $20-$30 million in renovations.

The DAC's membership—which was at 1,000 at the time, a 78 percent decrease from that peak in 1960—was also hit by the tragedy, as eleven of them died. The facility was closed for cleaning and the 2001 ceremony—the one in which Crouch received his award—would be moved from the fabled wood-paneled Heisman Room to the Marriott Marquis in Times Square, ending a sixty-seven-year run of announcements in its halls.

"The bottom line," James E. Corcoran, the club's president, wrote in a letter to the club's 900 members that November, "is that if our members living and working out together on Wall Street for the past 20 years cannot come up with a solution to this challenge, then we all know what the final outcome will be."

The plan was for the DAC to reopen in January, with a goal of expanding membership upward of 2,200, which could give the club $2.2 million to help pay its monthly mortgage. Compounding matters, the $8.3 million it borrowed to buy those bottom thirteen floors from Cheslock Bakker was due in August 2001.

"You'd think we could come up with a way to creatively finance it," Corcoran told the *New York Times* in November 2001. "But it's the whole asset-rich, cash-poor situation."

The truth was, clubs like the DAC were dinosaurs, links to a bygone era when its clientele used it for banquets and other events. In the current climate, it could no longer keep up with fitness chains that didn't require thousands a year in fees. The club laid off sixty-five of its seventy staffers and, losing $500,000 a month, had solicited helps from members, sending out 900 letters. Only 200 responded, and when it invited 500 to a meeting on the future of the DAC, only sixty were in attendance. In 2002, once again, the club declared bankruptcy.

US Senator Charles Schumer, D-NY., made a play to get the DAC, and other nonprofits, a share of $225 million in relief plan funds allocated by Congress, but to no avail. The DAC would never open its doors again.

On August 30, 2002, it failed to make its balloon payment. The club's floors were also in need of $10 million in repairs, and the developer that owned the rest of the building turned the DAC's floors into luxury condominiums called the Downtown Club.

An icon without a home, the trophy ceremony jumped from the Marriott Marquis to the Yale Club in 2002 (Carson Palmer's winning year) and '03 (Jason White) and the New York Hilton in '04 (Matt Leinart). That's the environment Crouch points to when he wonders "if the Heisman was going to be around," before it settled into its current hosting site, the PlayStation Theater (also called Nokia Theater Times Square from 2005–10 and Best Buy Theater from 2010–15).

Gone was the splendor of the DAC, its walls dripping with the words of decades worth of winners. The Trust tried to recapture some of that destination feel in a partnership with the Sports Museum of America, which had hopes of hosting the presentation before it went under in 2009. Now, the trophy's backers reside in an office building on Broadway near Wall Street, with a staff of two full-time employees—executive director Rob Whalen and coordinator Tim Henning. The Trust—all of whom work pro bono—oversees the operation.

It's a lean outfit, but the Heisman has survived, driven by two pillars: the award and its charity work.

"We have a dual mission," Dockery said. "Number one is to maintain the integrity of the trophy . . . and the second, which is almost as important as that to the trustees, is the charitable mission. To give something back, to be able to make some small contribution to the common good, which we do."

172

The Trust has made donations in excess of $7.5 million since 2004, benefitting over 200 registered 501(c)(3) tax-exempt nonprofit organizations, and since the 2006 Heisman weekend, that has also included former winners, who for their participation receive checks to pass along to foundations of their choosing.

"I've definitely taken advantage of that and given to nonprofits in the Omaha and Nebraska areas, which is just wonderful," Crouch said. "It's great. It's helping a lot of kids."

Through partnerships with the likes of ESPN, Nissan, and Wendy's as well as licensing deals, the Trust is generating more than $5.6 million annually.

"This is what the Heisman does in the offseason, is to work on the charitable portions of it," Dockery said. "We don't accept donations. We earn these monies that we give away."

That side of the Heisman has become magnified with the inclusion of the Heisman Humanitarian Award. Established in 2006, its recipients are sporting figures that have impacted communities, counting Olympian Joey Cheek ('06), soccer legend Mia Hamm ('09), NASCAR's Jeff Gordon ('12), and Hall of Fame baseball manager Joe Torre ('14) among its winners.

The intention wasn't to bring the charitable side of the trophy to the limelight as much as it was to show younger generations what's possible.

"Maybe encourage other people to say 'Marty Lyons ['11 winner] is doing this' or 'David Robinson ['13] is doing that,'" Dockery said, "'If they can find time and energy to do that, maybe I can do something on a smaller level.' So it's to encourage people to emulate them also."

The Heisman's recipients are doing that on their own. Charlie Ward ('97) works with the Booker T. Washington Quarterback Club, Doug Flutie's ('84) Flutie Foundation aids families affected by autism, and Tim Tebow ('07) has his own foundation that, among its work, helps children fighting terminal illnesses, offers adoption aid, and has held 200 proms for 32,000 people with special needs.

It's 1996 winner Danny Wuerffel, though, who has made charity his life's second act, and has benefitted from the Trust's donations. With parallels to the Heisman's own fight for survival, the former Florida quarterback's work has been a testament to perseverance.

"How do you leverage whatever sphere of influence you have and resources and talents to invest that in a purpose bigger than yourself?" Wuerffel said. "As a Heisman winner, there is a phenomenal platform that has been created and stewarded by others that I was honored to be included in and be a part of . . . so how do I steward that gift?"

Wuerffel isn't one to turn away when he feels he's being led toward something. During his playing days with the New Orleans Saints, he had heard of Desire Street Ministries—which was founded in 1990 by Mo Leverett to aid the 9th Ward neighborhood—from several people, then received a brochure in his mailbox.

"[I] was really fascinated with the mission and the vision," Wuerffel said of its stated goal "to love our neighbor by revitalizing impoverished neighborhoods through spiritual and community development." The idea was that Desire Street would begin with its own constituents and then expand its work to other areas in need.

He invited Leverett to speak to his teammates at a chapel service and in turn, the quarterback was asked to come to see the impoverished community. Wuerffel can still recall that eye-opening experience.

"I remember driving into the neighborhood the first time and was just really awestruck by how old the project buildings were," he said. "I couldn't believe, they looked like they were condemned and they should have been torn down years ago . . . and yet at the same time I saw a girl walk out of one of the doors carrying her little doll, and I realized that she still lived there."

Desire Street had established a church; a private school for boys, known as Desire Street Academy; a children's medical clinic; and community gardens. Wuerffel played his last NFL game in 2002, and two years later he began working full time with Desire Street, serving as the school's development director and helping with fund-raising. He saw himself as "really a supportive part of the piece."

Hurricane Katrina would alter Desire Street's plans and push Wuerffel to the forefront when it hit in August 2005. The group's $3 million facilities were located two blocks from the breach on the west side of the canal and it was submerged in eight feet of water, while the people it served scattered across the country as they lost their homes. Desire Street leadership had dealt with financial problems leading up to the storm, wondering whether they could make payroll—"Which wasn't too uncommon in the early years," Wuerffel said. But the community was exasperated by the hurricane.

Everything the staff had built had been destroyed.

"Our staff was really broken and shaken up as well," Wuerffel said, "and you put all those factors together and you do have to wonder, 'Is this something that was an amazing gift in the time that it existed and the lives that it impacted in those first fifteen years?'"

Wuerffel and his wife Jessica had made contact with eighty of the school's students, though one he was close with had not been located and many suspected he had not survived. "I just remember one feeling of being just like between a rock and a hard place," Wuerffel said. "I had the image from Exodus where Moses and the Israelites were up against the Red Sea and then you have this army coming at him and it was like, 'Man, if something doesn't happen, miraculously, we're stuck.'"

He heard word of a facility in the Florida panhandle at Camp Timpoochee that happened to be owned by the University of Florida, which Wuerffel had helped to win four straight SEC championships and the 1996 national title. He drove to Gainesville to speak to school officials and it was during that meeting that Desire Street Academy found its evacuation spot—in a town called Niceville, Florida.

"That became available, and just that whole experience, was incredibly overwhelming," Wuerffel said.

Leverett resigned in 2006 and Wuerffel took over as executive director, and while the school later set up in Baton Rouge, the state of the economy robbed it of the donations it needed to stay afloat and it closed its doors.

In the summer of 2015 construction began on Desire Community Square, an extension of the foundation that is to be run by local non-profits Abundance of Desire, Daughters of Charity, and Kids of Excellence. Meanwhile, Desire Street Ministries is now headquartered in Atlanta, but it hasn't lost its connection to New Orleans. It has moved forward with a twist on that vision of strengthening communities.

"The bigger question was, 'How do you grow? How do you expand?'" Wuerffel said. "That's where we did have a shift in that we decided not to start and run multiple Desire Street ministries that were kind of branded by us and managed and run by us."

Instead, it empowers. The ministry works with individuals across the country who are living in neighborhoods and supports them, taking advantage of the work they have already done instead of trying to start from scratch with their own people.

"I think it's a highly efficient investment of time and resources in that you don't have to recreate wheels," Wuerffel said. "Doing inner-city work, one of the biggest components is about being present and building trust and that takes a very long time, and to find people that have already been living in a neighborhood, some cases all their lives and in other cases, four, five, six years, they already earned some credibility in their neighborhood and some trust momentum.

"Usually at the same time there's a weariness. It's really, really hard work to live and serve in neighborhoods. There's so much need and what we find so often is people with great hearts and great intentions end up burning out, it's just overwhelming."

Desire Street—like the Heisman—has overcome. Its leader has overcome as well. In 2011, Wuerffel noticed he was losing sensation in his legs and arms after battling a stomach virus. He was diagnosed with Guillain-Barré Syndrome, a rare autoimmune disorder that causes paralysis. During his recovery, Wuerffel was advised to stay immobile.

At first, he had plans of binge-watching movies, but then he saw it as a unique opportunity for true personal reflection, devoid of distraction.

"Just sitting with whatever emotions come up and kind of going deep into your heart and soul was just really difficult and a beautiful time for my life," Wuerffel said. "[It] forced me to slow down, which is really, really hard to do these days, and I think it has led me into deeper places in my own soul, to discover parts of my life maybe I didn't want to admit existed, and really do my best to be a kind and humble person and define deeper parts of my life."

Through this process, he has come to more strongly embody the Heisman. Wuerffel did so as a player as the record-breaking face of Steve Spurrier's Fun n' Gun offensive evolution. Now, he's representing the other side of the trophy, that lesser known but maybe more impactful side.

"If I have five lives to live, there are several things I would consider doing with it," Wuerffel said, "but I believe as a Christian you have one life to live. . . . I like the language of 'you have one life to give.'"